"Robert Waldron gives us yet another luminous guide to poetry as a way of prayer and contemplation. His polestar for the journey this time is Thomas Merton, who was of course both a great poet and a great contemplative.

"For the novice, there isn't a more concise or powerful introduction to Merton's poetry. For the initiated, Waldron's analysis teems with fresh insight, invigorated by the author's profound faith and a lifelong experience of 'sapiential' reading.

"This new volume is biography, too; a vivid cameo portrait of Thomas Merton as monk, poet and celebrity. The reader will not only come to know the life of contemplation as revealed in Merton's verse, but also the contemplative gift that can be awakened in each of us by the way we read poetry, Merton's and others—a gift to help transform our lives, our relationship to the world and to God. This is an eloquent book of deepest spirituality and poetic understanding."

David Impastato, poet and author of Upholding Mystery:
An Anthology of Christian Poetry

"'Thomas Merton with rinsed eyes saw his world with wonder.' Robert Waldron's find book is awash with the same awe and simple attentiveness that form the heart of a poem or prayer. This gifted teacher examines Merton's poetry with sensitivity and contagious enthusiasm. Like Waldron's *Poetry as Prayer: The Hound of Heaven*, this study deserves a wide audience."

Jonathan Montaldo, Director, Thomas Merton Center,
Bellarmine College

"Robert Waldron's new book, *Poetry as Prayer: Thomas Merton* is a wonderful read and deserves a wide audience. The selected poetry of Thomas Merton as well as the commentary by the author helps prepare the spirit for contemplative prayer and to savor the things of God. An ideal book for a time of retreat or for anytime."

Brother Patrick Hart, OCSO,
Thomas Merton's secretary

Poetry as Prayer
Thomas Merton

Poetry as Prayer
Thomas Merton

by Robert Waldron

Artwork by Helen Kita

Pauline
BOOKS & MEDIA
BOSTON

Library of Congress Cataloging-in-Publication Data

Waldron, Robert G.
  Poetry as prayer: Thomas Merton / Robert Waldron ;
interpretive artwork by Helen Kita.
      p.cm. — (The poetry as prayer series)
  Includes bibliographical references.
  ISBN 0-8198-5919-2
      1. Merton, Thomas, 1915–1968—Criticism and interpretation.
2. Christian poetry, American—History and criticism. 3. Prayer
in literature. I. Title. II. Series.

PS3525.E7174 Z92 2000
811'.54—dc21

                                                    99-055540

Copyright © 2000, Daughters of St. Paul

Printed and published in the U.S.A. by Pauline Books & Media,
50 Saint Pauls Avenue, Boston, MA 02130-3491.

www.pauline.org.

Pauline Books & Media is the publishing house of the Daughters
of St. Paul, an international congregation of women religious
serving the Church with the communications media.

1 2 3 4 5 6   05 04 03 02 01 00

*Dedicated to
the memory of Thomas Kloss
1947–2000*

Contents

Foreword

As I began to harvest my thoughts on this gem of a book, I was pleasantly startled by the sudden realization that today, December 10, marks the date of Thomas Merton's entrance to Gethsemani as well as the date of his death. This moment of divine synchronicity gladdened my heart. How fitting to be praying his poetry on this day!

Thomas Merton, with his captivating, charming, baffling and complex personality, has become one of my most endearing mentors. I love him for his passionate search for union with God, his openness to learning and unlearning, his sense of humor, his holy restlessness and, finally, this faithfulness in struggling with the many seeming contradictory calls in his life. He lived in the cusp of light and darkness, silence and words, rest and restlessness, consolation and angst, solitude and community, writer and hermit, fame and obscurity, monk and social activist. In the end, these calls were not really so contradictory; each nourished the other along the way.

Among the many faces of Thomas Merton, the face of poet shines forth, brightly revealing itself not only in his poetry, but in all his writings as well. This is because Merton was a person extremely sensitive to beauty and truth, the stuff out of which poems are born.

I am delighted with the birth of *The Poetry as Prayer Series*. In this second volume of the series, Robert Waldron entices us to spend time with Merton the poet. Waldron's ten steps to reading poetry in a holy way, along with his eloquent meditative commentaries on three of Merton's poems, effectively portray how poetry can be prayer.

Waldron would have us read these poems as if we are on a quest for the mystery they hold. As he unveils his understanding of the meaning of each poem, we are ushered into the core of the poem's deep inner beauty. Praying these poems quite naturally lead me into a way of prayer much loved by monastics: *Lectio Divina*, the slow, reflective reading that calls us into profound listening to the Word of God. Thus, "Elias" becomes God's purifying Word for me as I sit in the "wilds" of my life, cradling my own brokenness, longing for the grace to trust the place where the path ends and the soul flies free.

In "Night-Flowering Cactus," I am lovingly imprisoned in the mysterious beauty of a darkness that tenderly holds my life. I have no way of finding myself, I realize. I can only lose myself in God that I may be found. All I know is that I *don't* know; thus I come to rely on the wisdom of waiting in darkness.

"Stranger" paints an icon with a few precious words, teaching me to see. Lured into the simplicity of mindfulness, I become aware that nothing is too small to behold. A simple gaze upon small things may reveal the One who holds and beholds me. My soul awakens as I am drawn into God and into my true self.

This is a book to pray rather than read. As I became immersed in its gentle spirit, my fondness for Merton deepened and I found myself wishing that I were one of Robert Waldron's students. I am particularly grateful for his notable gift of offering a short yet concise overview of Merton's life and his writings.

Treasure the gift you are holding as you begin to walk through these pages.

Be blessed!

Macrina Wiederkehr, OSB
St. Scholastica Monastery

Acknowledgements

Madonna Therese Ratliff, FSP
Brother Patrick Hart, OCSO
Brother Paul Quenon, OCSO
Rev. Matthew Kelty, OCSO

and

Jonathan Montaldo,
Director of the Thomas Merton Center,
Bellarmine College

Introduction

Poets are models *par excellence* of people who live in the "Now"; they are people who tingle with life. Their verse is charged with their life-force so that when we read it, we, too, are often charged with life. We promise ourselves to make greater effort to live more intensely our own "Now" moments. All poets in some fashion remind us, as the ancient poet Horace with his dictum, "carpe diem," that our time here on earth is not eternal, that we must "seize the day" every day.

When I was younger I turned to poetry, not so much to embrace immediate reality, but to escape it. Verse became a haven where I could abide with the poets. In my imagination I roamed the beautiful and haunting Lake District of England with William Wordsworth and his sister Dorothy. Samuel Taylor Coleridge's verse transported me to exotic and exciting dreamscapes which expelled all that was mundane and worrisome from their boundaries. For the sheer joy of language drenched in beauty, I could always turn to Shelley and Keats, their landscapes fraught with skylarks, autumnal beauty, and magical moonlight. For Arthurian romance I needed only to open Tennyson's "Idylls of the King" to become part of the realm of chivalry and damsels in distress.

Gerard Manley Hopkins' verse reminded me of life's holiness and God's abiding presence even during the dark night he illustrated in his terrible sonnets. Francis Thompson's gorgeous verse was a constant reminder of God's love for us, a love that "hounds" us to the ends of the earth. In my own spiritual aridity, I read Eliot's "Four Quartets," and believed that if he could successfully pass through the Waste Land, so, too, could I.

Poets offered me a saving word, the very word I desperately needed in order to face and overcome a problem, an anxiety, an inadequacy, or simply to get through the day. Its power, like a mantra, centers the soul. Suffice it to say that, without the poets, I might not have prevailed to be writing this introduction. There were so many poets who mysteriously appeared in my life to nourish my soul on both good and bad days. On second thought, perhaps their appearance is not so mysterious after all, because I believe God sends us the messengers we need.

And for me, because teaching literature is my vocation, God's messengers have most often been poets.

Now, as a person over age 50, I turn to poetry for different reasons. Rarely do I desire an escape from reality; on the contrary, I want to embrace it, to live acutely in the Present Moment in the manner of the mystics and poets.

I need poets to repeat "Pay attention!" until I learn to live attentively. I do not want to come to the end of my life and realize that I've not lived intensely, or as Henry David Thoreau would say, "deliberately." Like the poet Denise Levertov in her "Flickering Mind," I've been "absent" from too much of my life, too much from my true self, too much from God's presence in the world.

Often, when I read great (especially religious) poetry, I feel recharged and more alive. I feel as if a voltage of energy has electrified my spirit. The great poet of Carmel, California, Robinson Jeffers, suggests that poetry "is capable of affecting life directly; it sharpens the perceptions and emotions, and it can reconcile man to his environment or inspire him to change it."[1] In short, poetry helps us to live well.

So, unlike W. H. Auden who says poetry changes nothing, I believe that if we devote our attentive efforts to reading poetry, we will be richly rewarded. In his recent book, *Errata*, philosopher George Steiner writes, "often entirely unexpected…the poem or novel or play which, as it were, lay in ambush…the meeting, the collision between awareness and signifying form…is among the most powerful. It can transmute us."[2]

In fact, each time we engage a poem and plumb its meaning, we create an opportunity for epiphany in our lives: moments of soul-realization that can transfigure us. Thus, a close reading of a poem is a journey into our deepest selves, into the meaning of our lives. And what better companion to have on our life's journey than Thomas Merton, one of the greatest modern spiritual masters and also one of its finest religious poets. Merton deeply understood the power of verse, through contemplation, to bring us closer to God. Poets rely upon the *symbol* to transport their meaning because it transcends the ordinary. Thus we are offered a glimpse beyond the veil. Reading poetry also helps us to train our ability to focus; I firmly believe that *attention* is the secret of the contemplative life without which it is nearly impossible to be present to God.

I hope *Poetry as Prayer: Thomas Merton* leads you into a deeper prayer life and into a deeper appreciation of some of the finest verse ever written. In my previous book *Poetry as Prayer: The Hound of Heaven*, I said, "When entering the 'sacred ground' of poetry be prepared for anything to happen." This "anything" abides in the positive and life-enhancing order of things, and transformation is an ever-present possibility.

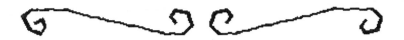

Chapter 1

Poetry as Contemplative Prayer

After thirty-six years of reading Thomas Merton's works, I finally visited the Abbey of Gethsemani where Merton had spent most of his adult life. I simply wanted to see where he had lived, to breathe the air that he had breathed, and to meet some of those who had known him. After beholding the center of his cenobitic and eremitical life, I thought that I might understand more deeply his vocation as a monk and poet.

While standing before his gravesite, I was greeted by a man in a T-shirt, pants that had seen better days, and a straw hat. He turned out to be a Trappist poet, Brother Paul Quenon. As we talked briefly about poetry, he seemed to read my mind. He told me that Thomas Merton had written his poem "Elias–Variations on a Theme" in a nearby red trailer left behind by a construction crew in the early 1950s—the very information I wanted verified for this book. The coincidence surprised me. He then offered to show me Merton's first hermitage, a tool shed he had named after Saint Anne. Later, Brother Patrick Hart (Merton's personal secretary) and Jonathan Montaldo (curator of the Merton Center, Bellarmine College) would bring me to his final hermitage.

Poetry and Place

Built of simple cinder block, this final hermitage was humble, inviting, secluded in a peaceful area. When I first saw it, I received a piercing insight: we all possess our own hermitage within. All of us have the power to enter into our souls simply by an act of attention; thus, we can pray anywhere; we can recall verses anywhere. If we are poets, we can be inspired anywhere. Revelation, like Merton's famous "Louisville Epiphany," can occur on the crowded corner of a busy city. We can, at will, enter what the Quaker mystic Thomas Kelly calls the "Divine Center." He says, "Deep within us all there is an amazing inner sanctuary of the soul, a holy place, a Divine Center, a speaking Voice, to which we may continuously return."[1]

So, does a monk have a better chance of experiencing the contemplative life than the average person? I can only speak from my own experience. Although I've been attracted to the monastic lifestyle for most of my life, I have had to accept the fact that my vocation is elsewhere. And after many years of teaching and reading poetry, I now realize that my life possesses many parallels to the life of the monk. Granted, I do not sing the Psalter every week or follow the Liturgy of the Hours daily, but I do follow my own *Lectio Divina*, or "sacred reading": my own personal reading and teaching of poetic texts, accomplished over the years with my students.

Thus, I was pleased to find Trappist Michael Casey's advising that the Psalms be read as one reads poetry:

> *Lectio Divina* is like reading poetry: we need to slow down, to savor what we read, and to allow the text to trigger memories and associations that reside below the threshold of awareness. We are so accustomed to reading quickly and "objectively" that we easily slip back into habit, even when we are reading purely for "subjective" profit. This means that we may have to make a stand to protect the specific character of holy reading.[2]

I can say with confidence that I have indeed lived a kind of monastic life in the world of my academic profession. During all those years, not only was I reading, but I was also praying some of the greatest poetry ever written.

Seeing this hermitage helped me to understand both Merton the contemplative and Merton the poet. It also confirmed for me the affinity between prayer and poetry.

Poetry's Purpose

Merton entered the Abbey of Gethsemani to, as he saw it, "disappear into God." Such an expression is an excellent poetic definition of contemplation; it is a kind of "disappearance" into God, if you will. Merton, who entered the monastery at 27 in 1941, was already a contemplative. By this I mean he had already been praying much of his life—although he very likely hadn't known it—by "disappearing" often into the reading and composing of poetry. The creative process demands a loss of the self before art can be brought to birth. Writing poetry prepared Merton for the Trappist life, for of its very nature creativity is already anchored in the contemplative life.

If you are a person who sets aside time in your life for reading and silent reflection, you have the right to describe yourself as a contemplative. Of course, losing yourself in a fast-paced mystery novel is not the same as losing yourself in Francis Thompson's *The Hound of Heaven* or the poetry of Thomas Merton or the Psalms. What's the difference? Poets have earned access to the depths of the human soul; they have paid strict attention to the movements of the spirit; they have plummeted to the very self, a locus many are afraid to behold. They relate their journey and offer the gems of wisdom they have won with language that is rhythmic, lyrical, and often symbolic.

Poets devote their lives to the act of finding, as Wallace Stevens says, "what will suffice." Being cartographers of the soul, they are searchers of meaning. John Paul II writes, "Every genuine art form in its own way is a path to the inmost reality of man and of the world. It is therefore a wholly valid approach to the realm of faith, which gives human experience its ultimate meaning."[3]

A common complaint, not only from my high school literature students, but also from friends, is that poetry intimidates them. "It's too hard to understand," say my students; "Modern poetry is too obscure," say my friends. They often add that they don't have the time to read poetry. Yes, some poetry is obscure and requires effort and time to understand. But consider for a moment where the poet has come from. This is a person who has struggled and made an inner journey and has arduously captured an experience in lovely language. Poems rarely appear full-blown from the soul; the poet must carve out a poem like the sculptor who carves his figures out of stone. John Paul II observes, "The particular vocation of individual artists decides the arena in which they serve, and points as well to the tasks they must assume, the hard work they must endure and the responsibility they must accept."[4]

A prayer-poem is often the fruit of an agonizing struggle to understand the meaning of one's life specifically, and life in general. We need only look at the lives of Gerard Manley Hopkins, T. S. Eliot, Robert Frost, and Sylvia Plath, to name a few, to understand how painful living as a poet can be. And if the poet is willing to embark on a painful inner journey and to share with others what has been discovered, then we should be willing to make the effort to understand that verse.

To penetrate the meaning of a poem requires that we surrender ourselves to the poem. While reading a poem, we can't be considering our vacation plans or thinking of our Christmas list at the same time. We must let go of life as we know it in order to enter into another's experience. We have to wear the poet's shoes, walk in the poet's footsteps. This requires humility. By entering the poet's experience we briefly give up our life in order to read and to meditate on another's life-rendering. During such times we say in effect: This poet's experience is worthy of exploration, and I may not only be nourished by its loveliness, but

I may also learn something about myself or be offered an insight that will help me to live my life. John Paul II says:

> Every genuine artistic intuition goes beyond what the senses perceive and, reaching beneath reality's surface, strives to interpret its hidden mystery. The intuition itself springs from the depths of the human soul, where the desire to give meaning to one's own life is joined by the fleeting vision of beauty and of the mysterious unity of things.[5]

Prayer takes us out of ourselves; it raises our hearts and minds. Prayer is attention. Prayer is wonder. Prayer is insight. Prayer is learning. Prayer is connection. Prayer is knowing and unknowing. Prayer is humility. Prayer affirms the importance of living our life well, according to our conscience.

Poetry also takes us out of ourselves. It raises our hearts and minds; it affirms life; it demands attention; it is founded in wonder and renews it; it offers insight into self-knowing; it teaches, connects and requires humility. In essence, poetry presents the possibility of a grace-full encounter with God. God "lures" us to himself through beauty. The Church has always appreciated art, whether it be the mysterious melodies of Gregorian chant, stained-glass windows that tell the story of Christ and the saints, or the architecture of Gothic cathedrals whose exquisite towers pierce the firmament, hinting at the human yearning for the Divine. Thus, a poem, too, may be the occasion for an encounter with grace, one that leads us, through faith, to a closer relationship with God.

God can reveal himself to us in any way he chooses, and he often does through beauty. Again, in his *Letter to Artists*, Pope John Paul II says:

> Beauty is a key to the mystery and a call to transcendence. It is an invitation to savor life and to dream the future.... It stirs that hidden nostalgia for God that a lover of beauty like Saint Augustine could express in incomparable terms: "Late have I loved you, beauty so old and so new: Late have I loved you!"[6]

Poetry and the Search for Meaning

Merton was an advocate of reading great literature, both prose and poetry, in a sapiential fashion. *Sapientia* is Latin for wisdom, and Merton believed that a wealth of wisdom was available to readers of the world's great literature. One need only read his literary essays on William Faulkner, or listen to the tapes of him teaching poetry to Gethsemani's novices to find confirmation of this approach.

In his beautiful essay "Baptism in the Forest: Wisdom

and Initiation in William Faulkner," Merton compares young Ike McCaslin's initiation as a hunter to every man's search for God. He also compares hunting to the monastic life. Monks are hunters: they hunt for God. Like any good hunter, monks follow the trail in search of signs, clues and telltale marks. They seek the vestiges (from *vestigum*, Latin for footprint) of God's presence.

Ike's life becomes a search for a bear named Old Ben. His continual mantra is "I must see him...I must look at him." When the young boy fails to find the bear, he realizes how unnecessarily encumbered he is by his gun, compass, watch, and stick. Once he has divested himself of these articles and returns to a more natural state, his desired vision is granted. While resting on a log, Ike's eyes fall on Old Ben's tremendous fresh footprints in the earth. Looking up slowly, he finally sees the bear. It seemed to appear from nowhere. Ike neither planned the sighting, nor could he have predicted it. When he least expected it simply happened, and he is reduced to awe.

Over the next four years, Ike sees the bear twice more. Both times he has a gun in his hands and yet, twice he "fails" to kill the bear. His search for Old Ben and his "inability" to shoot the animal puzzles and disturbs the teenager. He turns to his father for advice. Ike's father understands him. He understands his spiritual dilemma. When words of solace and wisdom fail to enlighten Ike, his father *reaches toward his shelf and takes down a volume of John Keats's poetry* and proceeds to read "Ode on a Grecian Urn" aloud to his son. The wise father knows that his son is grappling with the "Eternal Verities": issues of pity and truth, beauty and liberty, humility and pride. Reading the poem twice, the father asks his son, "Do you see now?" The boy is slow to answer, for he is stunned by the "shock of recognition." Hearing the poem spoken aloud is like vocal prayer. After some reflection Ike responds, "Yes, sir." It is through a listening—of both ear and heart—to the *beauty of poetry whose resonance is that of prayer*, that Ike achieves insight into the meaning of his hunting and into the purpose of his life.

To understand the profound matters of life, from time immemorial, we have *turned to our poets* for solace, comfort, insight, and wisdom. Reading literature (both prose and poetry) in a sapiential fashion helps us to live our lives, to find the footprints, which do not stop at the "overwhelming questions," but lead on to the insights needed in the face of such questions.

We live in an extremely fast-paced world. These days, in the wake of today's instantaneous communication, post office delivery is referred to as "snail mail." E-mail, computers, mobile phones, the internet…all of these modern conveniences condition us to live our lives in a constant state of rush. This may help to explain why "road rage" has become a national phenomenon, and why people are sometimes provoked by the normal delay of a red street light.

Why mention all this? Because reading poetry could be the very spiritual exercise we need to slow us down. A volume of poetry is, for the modern reader, a monastic cell that can be entered at any time. The reader's *Lectio Divina* is the poetic text; the white space on the page that envelops the verse is emblematic of the silence and solitude that poetry fosters in our lives. And when we put ourselves in the right frame of mind, choosing poetry worthy of our close reading, then our reading of verse becomes meditation—it becomes prayer.

Even if poetry merely brings quiet and peace into our lives, then our reading of poetry has flowered beyond ordinary possibilities and placed us in an innocent space beyond violation. And, like the young Ike who came upon the bear unawares, perhaps someday we will find ourselves in the presence of a divine vestige gifted to us by a poem—one that will indeed lead us toward the divine *Logos*, the Word beyond all words.

Chapter 2

Thomas Merton: Monk and Poet

Childhood and Youth

Thomas Merton was born on January 31, 1915, in Prades, France to an American mother with Quaker leanings and a New Zealander father who belonged to the Church of England. His parents were artists who had met in Paris as art students. His mother, Ruth Jenkins, was an independent, novel-thinking woman who supported pacifism and had a great desire for simplicity in living. For a woman of the early twentieth century, she had modern ideas about raising children. She kept a close eye on Merton and recorded everything about her son in "Tom's Book."

Ruth frequently photographed her son; one photo in particular seems to foreshadow the solitary monk her son would one day become. In it, the young child sits alone at a table with an open book before him. Both mother and son possessed stubborn personalities. Once, when the

5-year-old Tom refused to spell the pronoun *which* with an "h," Ruth sent her little preschooler to bed early.

Ruth Jenkins Merton died of cancer when Merton was 6 years old. Her death presents a poignant scene from Merton's childhood: the little boy received a letter from his mother informing him that he would never see her again. And, as his mother was dying in Bellevue Hospital, the boy was forced to wait outside in a car as it rained. Some think it was heartless of his mother to not see her child one last time; others think that she was only trying to spare her son a horrific scene. Nevertheless, Merton once said that solitaries (like himself) were likely formed by severe mothers.

Thereafter, Merton was raised, in turn, by either his maternal grandparents or his father. As a child he had little religious training, although his paternal grandmother managed to teach him the "Our Father." Merton's father was a truly gifted painter who enjoyed brief success. In 1928, Owen Merton and his 13-year-old son moved to England where Thomas was to live for the next seven years. There, he attended Oakham School and exhibited such a flair for languages he won a scholarship to Clare College, Cambridge University. At Oakham, he was also exposed to a "secular" kind of religion passed on by one of his teachers. Of this Merton wrote, "His religious teaching consisted in more or less vague ethical remarks, an obscure mixture of ideals of English gentle-manliness and his favorite notions of personal hygiene."[1]

Merton only attended Cambridge for a year, and did not distinguish himself academically. Perhaps this was partly due to his father's death of brain cancer in 1931; after this Merton's life was unhappy and often undisciplined. His unsupervised life as an undergraduate at Cambridge allowed him to indulge in much partying and drinking. Had his father lived, perhaps Merton would not have adopted such a riotous lifestyle. The day after his nineteenth birthday, on January 31, 1934, Merton embarked on a vacation to Italy—a journey that would transform him forever.

Merton the Pilgrim

In his autobiography, *The Seven Storey Mountain*, Merton calls himself a pilgrim while he was in Rome. Although unaware of it at the time, he truly was a pilgrim in the original meaning of the word: one who visits religious shrines. Touring Roman churches, Merton was fascinated by Byzantine mosaics, and discovered them to be not only beautiful, but spiritually powerful. He eagerly went from church to church to gaze upon the iconic splendor of mosaics and stained glass windows: Saints Cosmas and Damian, Saint Maria Maggiore, Saint Sabina, the Lateran, Saint Costanza, Saint Prudenziana and Saint Praxeds.

At first it was the beauty of these saint-mosaics that enthralled him. Later, the huge icons of Christ overwhelmed him, jerked him out of himself so that, for the first time in his life, he desired to know, "who this Person was that men called Christ." It seems that the figure of Christ himself beckoned Merton through ecclesiastical art. This serves as a bridge to the divine as confirmed by the French mystic, Simone Weil, whom Merton came to admire later in his life. Weil writes, "In everything which gives us the pure, authentic feeling of beauty, there is, as it were, an incarnation of God in the world, and it is indicated in beauty."[2]

Mesmerized by the spiritual power of Christian iconography, Merton haunted these ancient Roman churches and their treasures. To understand and learn more about their main subject, Jesus Christ, Merton purchased a Vulgate Bible and immediately began to read and study it. Certainly these actions are part of Merton's conversion experience, but only the very beginning of a conversion. His actual rebirth in the waters of Baptism, and the desire to live the Catholic faith, were still a long way off.

One night in a hotel room in Rome, Merton unexpectedly felt the presence of his recently departed father, whom he missed terribly. He wrote of the experience:

> I was in my room. It was night. The light was on. Suddenly it seemed to me that father, who had now been dead more than a year, was there with me. The sense of his presence was as vivid and as real and as startling as if he had touched my arm or spoken to me...instantly I was overwhelmed with a sudden and profound insight into the misery and corruption of my soul, and I was pierced deeply with a light that made me realize something of the condition I was in...and now I think for the first time in my whole life I really began to pray.[3]

But the impulse to pray proved short-lived. Merton returned to England and lived just as he had before, though on a much deeper level. He truly was not the same young man—something that would become more evident only later in America.

After Merton returned from Rome, Tom Bennet—

the man Owen Merton, shortly before his death, appointed as Thomas' guardian—advised the young Merton to leave England and live with his grandparents in New York. By this time Merton had fathered a son and had earned the reputation as a "wild youth." Thus, his original plan of procuring a job in the British Civil Service became very unlikely. Merton welcomed the opportunity to start anew in America. He enrolled at Columbia University in February of 1935.

Merton at Columbia University

Columbia was an exciting place for Merton both socially and intellectually. He made friends quickly and became a big name on campus. He involved himself in a number of activities: he was editor of the 1937 *Yearbook* and art editor of the Columbia University magazine, the *Jester*. His friends included Robert Lax, Robert Giroux, and Edward Rice. He attended classes taught by the well-known poet and critic Mark Van Doren who became Merton's friend and mentor.

At the same time, however, Merton still described himself as an agnostic and was hostile to formal religion. Haunted as he was with a sense of guilt for his past sexual life, and plagued by self-hate, he was acutely sensitive to the power of evil in the world. Despite his outward success, he often felt overwhelmed by the emptiness of his life and constantly searched for something to fill it. Perhaps in part this is why he continued to be a voracious reader. One day he saw Etienne Gilson's, *The Spirit of Medieval Philosophy*, displayed in Scribner's window on Fifth Avenue. He bought a copy and began reading it on the train home. But, he nearly threw it out a window when he noticed the *Nihil Obstat* and *Imprimatur*—proclaiming the Catholic Church's approval of the volume's contents.

The book, however, soon engaged Merton and at last introduced him to a concept of God that he found intellectually satisfying. God was not an enraged autocrat out to condemn as many people as possible. Rather, he was a loving and compassionate God. At about the same time, Merton also began reading books by the Catholic theologian and philosopher, Jacques Maritain, who introduced him to the idea of virtue. He also read books by the English essayist and novelist, Aldous Huxley, whose writings introduced him to mysticism.

Merton continued his former study of William Blake's poetry, as well as that of Dante and Gerard Manley Hopkins. All these writers played some part in very gradually, and yet persistently, "singing him"—as he phrased it—into the Catholic Church. It was while he read G. F. Leahy's biography of Gerard Manley Hopkins that Merton, impressed with the account of Hopkins's conversion to Catholicism through John Henry Newman's influence, decided on the spot that it was time to take instruction to become a Catholic. On November 18, 1938, Merton was baptized at Corpus Christi church in New York City.

The Searching Continues

When Merton was awarded his master's degree in February, 1939, he decided to leave his grandparents and to go out on his own. He rented an apartment on Perry Street, Greenwich Village, New York. In his newly-baptized fervor, Merton bought his first volume of the works of Saint John of the Cross. His reading material also included Saint Teresa of Avila's *Autobiography*, Thomas a Kempis' *Imitation of Christ*, Saint Augustine's *Confessions*, and Saint Ignatius of Loyola's *Spiritual Exercises*.

Merton was particularly taken with the Spanish mystics. Later in life, he would turn to the optimism of Julian of Norwich, an English mystic. Of her Merton later wrote: "Julian is without doubt one of the most wonderful of all Christian voices...whereas in the old days, I used to be crazy about Saint John of the Cross, I would not exchange

Julian for him now if you gave me the world and the Indies and all the Spanish mystics rolled up in one bundle."[4]

During these post-Columbia years, Merton was involved in several kinds of writing: keeping a journal, writing novels, and composing poetic verse. Although a new convert, Merton did not completely abandon his former lifestyle; he still partied, drank, and dated numerous women. And his dissatisfaction with life also persisted; something was lacking.

Merton first entertained the idea of becoming a priest when his friend and teacher, Dan Walsh, remarked that he thought Merton had a vocation to the priesthood. Walsh introduced Merton to the Franciscans. They were quite taken by the very personable and obviously brilliant young man. Over the next two years Merton began to envision himself as a Franciscan. Overwhelmed by scrupulosity of conscience, however, he informed them about his former life and of the child he had fathered. The Franciscans then advised him to withdraw his application. This request devastated Merton who had begun to sincerely believe himself called to the religious life. Because of this refusal, Merton thought he could never become a priest.

To uplift Merton's spirits, Walsh suggested that he

attend a retreat at the Trappist Abbey of Gethsemani in Kentucky. At Gethsemani during the Holy Week of 1941, Merton unexpectedly found what he had been searching for: "This is the center of America," he marveled. "I had wondered what was holding the country together, and what was keeping the universe from cracking in pieces and falling apart."[5]

Merton renewed his vocational discernment and returned to his new job, teaching literature at Saint Bonaventure College in New York. There he was introduced to Catherine de Hueck Doherty, also known as "The Baroness" because of her aristocratic Russian background. She had founded "Friendship House," a community of lay Catholics in Harlem whose purpose was to reach out to poor African-Americans. Merton now found himself pulled in two directions: to offer his life to the service of the poorest of the poor, or to become a Trappist monk. One inner voice asked, "Should I go to Harlem?" Another kept repeating, "Give up everything, give up everything!" In the end, Merton's monastic call was confirmed in a rather pragmatic way when he learned that the Trappists did not consider his fathering a child as an impediment to the priesthood. Merton cast his indecision aside and entered the Abbey of

Gethsemani on December 10, 1941. On December 13, 1941 he became a postulant choir monk.

Gethsemani

Merton's new life as a monk was the antithesis of modern twentieth-century life. He was now living in an ambiance of medieval silence, solitude, asceticism, and prayer according to the monastic tradition of *Lectio Divina*. Choir monks, dressed in white robes and black scapulars, devoted their days to the ancient maxim of *Ora et Labora* (prayer and work), while brown-clad lay brothers tended to much of the monastery's huge farm. It was a hard life, but one that enthralled the young man who felt he had at last found his true home.

Merton lived in a long dormitory divided into cells by partitions with only a curtain for a door. This allowed for little privacy. Each cell contained a wooden bed frame with a straw mattress, a crucifix, and stoup of holy water. The monks' vegetarian diet prohibited meat, fish, and eggs. During the seasons of Advent and Lent, the monks fasted more strictly. That winter of 1941, Merton lived according to the following schedule:

2:00 A.M.   Rise and go to choir for Matins and Lauds

2:30 A.M.   Meditation

3:00 A.M.   Night Office

5:30 A.M.	Prime, followed by Chapter
7:45 A.M.	Tierce, High Mass, Sext
11:07 A.M.	None
11:30 A.M.	Dinner
4:30 P.M.	Vespers
5:30 P.M.	Collation (light refreshment)
6:10 P.M.	Compline and Salve Regina
7:00 P.M.	Retire

Despite the rigors and the discipline of his new life, Merton's first enthusiasm to "disappear into God" was challenged early on by his personal reality. To his dismay, he soon realized that he had brought what he called his shadow, his writer-self, into Gethsemani. For Merton writing, or even the desire to write, seemed to be incompatible with his desire for God alone. Especially while writing poetry, Merton was unable to dispel the notion that he was disregarding the aims of his Cistercian vocation that demanded a greater and greater silence in his contemplative life. The guilt arose from the amount of time required for composing good verse; time set aside for poetry seemed to leave less time for contemplation. But Gethsemani's abbot was aware of Merton's talent; under his orders Merton continued to write poetry and began work on his autobiography. Only gradually, as

Merton realized how similar the poet's contemplation is to the monk's because both are rooted in God, did he pursue poetry free of a feeling of guilt.

His volume of poetry, *Thirty Poems,* was published in 1944. This was followed by another collection of verse in 1946: *A Man in the Divided Sea.* Twelve more volumes of verse would subsequently appear. Merton's poetic opus is quite substantial, especially when one considers the writing he accomplished in many other genres during his relatively short life (he died at age 53). His verses serve as a kind of poetic autobiography, a symbolic account of his inner journey as a monk, priest, poet, and philosopher. The following is a list of his poetry volumes:

1944	*Thirty Poems*
1946	*A Man in the Divided Sea*
1947	*Figures for an Apocalypse*
1949	*Tears of the Blind Lion*
1957	*The Strange Islands*
1959	*Selected Poems*
1962	*Original Child Bomb*
1963	*Emblems of a Season of Fury*
1966	*Sensation Time at the Home*
1968	*Cables to the Ace*

Merton's *The Seven Storey Mountain* was published in 1948, and to everyone's surprise, it became a worldwide bestseller. Merton became a celebrity.

Merton the Writer

In the 1950s Merton was, along with Fulton Sheen, America's most well-known Catholic. But, with this fame there arrived new problems for Merton to face, the most critical of which was the secular world's invasion of his silence and solitude. Merton had entered Gethsemani to "disappear into God." His fame, however, prevented this. His constant writing, with the concomitant "rewards" of fame—countless letters, demands for essays, articles, endorsements, sponsorships of a host of contemporary issues from Civil Rights to the nuclear arms race—all took its toll on his health. In September 1950, Merton entered a Louisville hospital where he was treated for exhaustion and colitis.

In 1951 Merton was made Master of Scholastics, a position of directing the young monks who were preparing for priesthood. It was work he enjoyed; having been a monk for ten years, he was in a position to evaluate his own life and to help others along the same path. During this time, he was also writing at a breathtaking pace. The 1950s saw the publication of more than a dozen books and a host of essays and reviews. In 1953 he published his most popular personal journal, *The Sign of Jonas*. His pivotal work on spirituality, *No Man Is an Island*, was published in 1955. Around this same time, Merton's hunger for solitude drew him to the idea of living in his own hermitage; and in 1955 he was given permission to use the monastery's forest lookout tower as an occasional hermitage.

On March 18, 1956, Merton went to Louisville on an errand. There Merton experienced his now famous "Louisville Epiphany" while standing on the corner of Fourth and Walnut Streets observing the busy crowds. In his journal *Conjectures of a Guilty Bystander*, he wrote about this revelation:

> In Louisville, at the corner of Fourth and Walnut, in the center of the shopping district, I was suddenly overwhelmed with the realization that I loved all those people, that they were mine and I theirs, that we could not be alien to one another even though we were total strangers. It was like waking from a dream of separateness, of spurious self-isolation in

a special world, the world of renunciation and supposed holiness. The whole illusion of separate holy existence is a dream.... Thank God, thank God that I am like other men, that I am only a man among others.[6]

The above clearly demonstrates that Merton was moving away from the petulant ascetic monk of his early years and toward becoming the radical humanist whose wide embrace of the world would appear full-blown in the 1960s. Merton emerged in the mid-1950s as an open-hearted monk fully alive to, and compassionate with, the world's woes.

A scrutiny of Merton's writings after his "Louisville Epiphany" also illustrates a prolific creativity. His poetic output alone tripled, and his newly found inclusiveness found expression in a myriad of essays on war, peace, non-violence, racism, the Cold War, arms control, and Eastern mysticism. Interestingly, it was during this time that Merton reworked an earlier essay, "Poetry and Contemplation," and published it in October, 1958. Clearly, he was coming nearer to integrating the two sides of his personality: contemplative and poetic.

Merton's writing positioned him at the forefront of

the 1960s American counter-revolution. To understand the depth of his involvement, one need only look at the titles of his poems written during those years: "The Moslem's Angel of Death," "An Elegy for Ernest Hemingway," "Elegy for James Thurber," "And the Children of Birmingham," "Chant to be Used in Processions Around a Site with Furnaces," "News from the School at Chartres," and "Hagia Sophia." These are not the poems of a world-denying monk, but those of a man committed to communicating with everyone regardless of religion, race, political persuasion or gender. The themes of his poems are as varied and complex as the issues of racism, the holocaust and feminine spirituality.

Merton the Hermit

Perhaps the most singular event for Merton in this decade was his permanent move into a hermitage, a permission granted reluctantly by his Abbot in 1965. He moved in on August 20, the Feast of Saint Bernard. Notwithstanding Merton's success, both as a monk and as a writer, he continued to feel a certain sense of restlessness. He truly believed that he needed to be away from the noisy upkeep of the monastery's huge farm, which he viewed as an obstacle to the silence he craved.

Merton hoped this move would protect and ensure his silence and solitude. But, like any "escape," however noble the reasons, the hermitage did not prove to be the paradise of his dreams. He missed communal life more than he expected, and he suffered from a crushing loneliness. As he soon learned, he seemed to be a person who worked best within an externally imposed structure, although, to his credit, Merton observed the following schedule during his hermitage years:

2:15 A.M.	Rise, Lauds, meditation
5:00 A.M.	Breakfast
5:30 A.M.	Prayer, study, and spiritual reading
7:30 A.M.	Prime, then rosary
8:00 A.M.	Manual work, chores, etc.
9:30 A.M.	Terce
10:30 A.M.	Sext
11:00 A.M.	None
11:30 A.M.	To the monastery for private Mass (until an altar was installed in the hermitage) thanksgiving, reading from the Psalter, dinner
1:00 P.M.	Vespers, followed by meditation
2:15 P.M.	Writing, work or walk
4:15 P.M.	Vigils anticipated

5:00 P.M.	Supper, followed by Compline
6:00 P.M.	New Testament reading, meditation, examination of conscience
7:00 P.M.	Retire

Still, the "hermitage years" were busy ones. Merton, taking the Church at her word, responded to Vatican II by reaching out to other religions in his writings with the hope that such dialogue would contribute to world unity and peace. Several books on Zen were published: *Mystics and Zen Masters* (1967), *Zen and the Birds of Appetite* (1968), as well as his "renderings" or translations of the Chinese sage, Chuang Tzu, *The Way of Chuang Tzu* (1965).

Although Merton considered himself a hermit, he did not have the heart to refuse the many visitors who asked to meet with him. These were often scholars, peace activists, and theologians. He entertained people as varied as the theologian and philosopher Jacques Maritain, the poet Denise Levertov, and the folk singer Joan Baez. He also continued to maintain a prodigious correspondence with such people as the founder of the Catholic Worker movement, Dorothy Day; the peace activist, James Forrest; the psychologist, Erich Fromm; the Polish poet, Czeslaw Milosz; and the Buddhist, Daisetz T. Suzuki.

While living in his hermitage, Merton received an

invitation to travel to Bangkok, Thailand, to speak at a conference on the Eastern and Western monastic experience. *The Asian Journal of Thomas Merton* records the author's fascination with the East, his admiration for Eastern spirituality, and his meeting with the Dalai Lama who was deeply impressed by Merton's spirituality.

Merton also experienced a profound epiphanic moment while standing before the huge stone, Buddhas of Polonnaruwa. He writes, "Looking at these figures, I was suddenly, almost forcibly, jerked clean out of the habitual, half-tied vision of things. An inner clearness, clarity, as if exploding from the rocks themselves, became evident and oblivious."[7] Kipling had once said that the East and West would never meet. As he stood in his bare feet before a shrine of the East, the Christian monk, Thomas Merton, proved him wrong. Merton's belief in the mystic way, both Eastern and Western Christian, was confirmed, as was his commitment to searching for common ground between the great religions of the world, in an effort toward dialogue among all peoples.

In Bangkok, on December 10, 1968, Merton gave his final talk at the conference, a paper titled "Marxism and Monastic Perspectives," on the transformation of the self as the goal of the monastic journey. He retired to his room in the late afternoon. Later, emerging from a shower, he touched the fan near his bed, and was electrocuted by 220 volts of electricity. His body was found later. He was flown back to America on a plane that also carried the bodies of American soldiers killed in the Vietnam War. The irony was sadly eloquent, for he was well known for his vocal opposition to this war.

Thomas Merton lies buried in the monks' cemetery at the Abbey of Gethsemani.

CHAPTER 3

From Merton's Pen

Many people who are new to Thomas Merton are overwhelmed by the number of books he wrote, in what seems to be every genre, and the several biographies now available. The often-heard question is: "Where do I start?" Perhaps the best place to begin is with *The Seven Storey Mountain*, one of the greatest autobiographies of this century.

This is where my own Merton journey began, and then I moved on to his popular books on the spiritual life: *Seeds of Contemplation*, *No Man Is an Island*, and *New Seeds of Contemplation*. I became fascinated by the monk behind these devotional books, and I took up *The Sign of Jonas*, a journal that remained my favorite Merton book for years because it took me inside the Abbey of Gethsemani where I could live Merton's life as a Trappist monk vicariously. It also describes the tension Merton experienced as a contemplative and a poet, a duality that for a long time he believed incompatible in his life as a monk. *The Sign of Jonas* narrates Merton's spiritual development as a monk and beautifully captures what it meant for him to be a priest. For an intimate portrait of Merton the monk, the poet, and the priest, this is the journal to read. The "inward gaze" he makes, addresses Merton's inner life within the Abbey of Gethsemani. *Conjectures of a Guilty Bystander* is Merton's journal of the "outward gaze"; in it he turns his attention upon the world and its various problems: racism, war, the Cold War, nuclear arms, politics, civil rights, Vietnam, etc. The title suggests Merton's belief that he stood by aloof from the world far too long and, consequently, must live with the resulting guilt. *Conjectures* addresses this existential guilt, chronicling Merton's movement from a monk focused primarily on his own salvation to that of a monk now open to and deeply concerned about the world's spiritual and physical suffering. Merton's emerging social consciousness comes to light, as well as his thoughts on the many books he was reading. Merton's insights into other writers are intriguing. He possessed an acutely sensitive inner radar with regard to this century's great writers, and his judgments have stood the test of time.

Speaking to a chapter of the International Merton Society, Basil Pennington, a Cistercian monk and biographer of Merton, recommended that the best way to get to know Merton was to read his letters. These letters are now published in five volumes: *The Hidden Ground of Love*, *The Road to Joy*, *The Courage for Truth*, *The School of Charity*, and *Witness to Freedom*. Apparently, there was no mask between Merton and his letters, which were often written quickly and spontaneously. Reading them is an illuminative experience; they offer a multifaceted portrait of a complex and often enigmatic personality.

There are several collections of Merton's essays to choose from. As a teacher of literature, I am most drawn to the *Literary Essays of Thomas Merton*, especially his essays on the French novelist Albert Camus, and on William Faulkner. Another collection, *Disputed Questions*, contains insightful meditations on the relationship between the contemplative and the secular world. It also includes "Philosophy of Solitude," an essential essay for understanding Merton as poet, written in the mid-1950s. The collection of essays, *Raids on the Unspeakable*, contains one of Merton's most haunting pieces, "Rain and the Rhinoceros." This exquisite prose poem equals Merton's lovely "Firewatch" found at the end of *The Sign of Jonas*.

Before attempting Merton's poetic verse, it would be helpful to have a brief overview of his most popular books: *Seeds of Contemplation*, *No Man Is an Island*, *Thoughts in Solitude*, and *The Living Bread*, as well as an introduction to Merton as poet. A word on ourselves as "readers" of poetry, and a chance to practice praying a poem prepare us for Merton's poems to come: "Elias–Variations on a Theme," "Night-Flowering Cactus," and "Stranger."

Seeds of Contemplation

Writer Paul Wilkes calls *Seeds of Contemplation* (published in 1949) Thomas Merton's greatest prose work and says it deserves to take its place among the world's great devotional books, alongside such classics as: *The Imitation of Christ*, *The Cloud of Unknowing*, *The Dark Night of the Soul*, *Practice of the Presence of God*, and *Revelations of Divine Love*.[1]

The America of the 1950s was ripe for a book such as *Seeds of Contemplation*. Many Americans, both Catholic and Protestant, were ready to embark on an inner journey. They had seen the atrocities of Nazism and the shocking agony caused by the bombing of Nagasaki and Hiroshima. Humanity had unleashed a destructive force powerful enough to destroy the world; thus, the late

1940s and the decade of the 1950s became an "Age of Anxiety" under the Cold War's threat of worldwide nuclear destruction.

When Thomas Merton appeared on the literary scene with his writings about the spiritual life, America was hungry for his message. Readers found Merton endearing; they saw that he was, like themselves, a vulnerable and complex man, far from perfect, and willing to share with others his interior journey. If the world lacked peace, he said, then men must seek it within themselves. And the path to the inner self was the way of contemplation.

We should remember that Merton himself had only recently become aware of the real meaning of the word *contemplation*. And this newness colored the uniqueness of his approach: he was willing to humbly share everything he learned about the spiritual life with his readers. His efforts to become a contemplative were made intimate by the very nature of his journalistic style of writing. Merton wrote from the heart, which was the way he spoke: person to person, devoid of jargon and obscurity.

Merton himself described *Seeds* as "nothing more than a collection of notes and personal reflections."[2] Readers felt comfortable with Merton's implicit promise that the contemplative experience was not some kind of Mount Everest available only to spiritual athletes—monks and other privileged souls—but available to all Christians who truly desired to know God.

Perhaps the most important aspect of *Seeds* is Merton's theory of the false and true self. He wrote, "Every one of us is shadowed by an illusory person: a false self." This image of the self, Merton asserts, is one that "exists only in my own egocentric desires."[3] Our true self is anchored in Christ. The more Christ-like we become, the more we are our true selves.

Merton's preoccupation with the false and the true self took root in the tendency among his many readers to canonize the young man in the early stages of his vocation as a monk and writer. In fact, after the publication of *The Seven Storey Mountain,* such notable figures as Evelyn Waugh, Grahame Greene, and Clare Booth Luce heaped praise upon Merton, while young men flocked to Gethsemani to emulate their newfound hero by becoming monks.

Many people viewed Merton as a modern prophet, a role Merton felt uncomfortable with. He feared he might be presenting a false self to the world when writing about the spiritual life. In addition, Merton was young. He had been baptized a Catholic when he was twenty-three, had entered Gethsemani at age 27, and had been a monk only three years when he began writing his autobiography and only six years when he began *Seeds of Contemplation*. There were many holy monks at Gethsemani who had lived the contemplative life long before Merton, and yet here was a novice claiming to be one of the proficients! Naturally there was some resentment from a few of Gethsemani's monks, but when Merton set forth his theory of the false self, he had himself in mind above all.

Seeds of Contemplation also presents an important turning point in Merton's own spiritual life. When he first entered Gethsemani, Merton was to some degree an isolationist: he felt the world was evil and was fleeing it before he became too ensnared. By the time he wrote *Seeds*, a new altruism replaced his former *contemptus mundi* (contempt for the world). He writes, "I must look for my identity somehow, not only in God but in other men."[4] This statement proves that he had gained the wisdom to understand that an inner journey that fails to move lovingly toward others is a journey that dead-ends in narcissism.

It must be kept in mind, however, that Merton's *Seeds* is the book of a young Catholic convert, and is imbued with the intense ardor of one newly baptized into the fold. While admiring the work, Paul Wilkes also remarks that it is "far too triumphalist."[5] Merton himself rated his book as "youthful; too simple, too crude," and it is not surprising that, in 1962, he completed a new edition of *Seeds* and called it *New Seeds of Contemplation*. Merton felt the first work to be too narrow, too judgmental, and too focused on the monastic life. *New Seeds* shows Merton far more aware of the modern world and its needs. It also illustrates Merton's growing awareness that the whole (holy) person is one who is able to integrate the inward gaze with the outward gaze. Therefore, Merton was concerned not only with his personal salvation, but also the salvation of his world-wide brothers and sisters.

No Man Is an Island

No Man Is an Island is a sequel to *Seeds of Contemplation*, and tells us in no uncertain terms that Merton, like John Donne, is indeed "involved in mankind." His involvement is that of calling everyone to a deeper spiritual life, and more specifically, to follow one's vocation: "Every man has a vocation to be someone, but he must understand clearly that in order to fulfill this vocation he can only be one person: himself."[6] Paradoxically, the only way we can truly be ourselves is to lose ourselves in Christ. Thus, "no man is an island" simply means, in theological terms, that we are all members of the mystical body of Christ.

Although *No Man Is an Island* is intended to foster the interior life, there is a startling passage that reminds us all that as we do so, we continue to live in this world:

> One of the most important—and most neglected—elements in the beginnings of the interior life is the ability to respond to reality, to see the value and the beauty in ordinary things, to come alive to the splendor that is all around us in the creatures of God…. The first step in the interior life is not, as some might imagine, learning *not* to see and taste and hear and feel things. On the contrary, what we must do is begin by unlearning our wrong ways of seeing, tasting, feeling, and so forth, and acquire a few of the right ones.[7]

The above is in keeping with Merton the poet who, along with William Blake, believes that "Everything that is / Is holy." Clearly Merton desires to be sensitive to all that is present in and of the world in the Holy Now; consequently, his highly developed inward gaze embraces an ever expanding outward gaze. For Merton, prayer includes gazing upon the beauty which is the divine smile presented by God to lure souls to himself, but it also includes seeing and empathizing with the suffering of our fellow brothers and sisters in Christ. And to love them we must allow them to be who they are.

No Man Is an Island is essentially a book about loving and forgiving. Love begins with the self. Christians must strip themselves of all that is false and hypocritical in order to love that which is their true self: the Christ within. The awakening of the true self permits all Christians to say with Paul "I live now, not I, but Christ lives in me" (Gal 2:20).

Thoughts in Solitude

Thoughts in Solitude is a quiet, wise book about the need for solitude and silence in our lives. Merton offers his readers "fundamental intuitions" about solitude because he has accepted the call to a vocation in which solitude was an integral part of his life.

We all, Merton says, contain within ourselves our own desert place of silence and solitude. We must not be afraid of this lonely space; in fact, once we accept our solitariness, we are on our way to realizing that we are indeed not alone, for God is with us. Merton says, "Solitude has to be objective and concrete. It has to be a communion in something greater than the world, as great as being itself, in order that in its deep peace we may find God."[8] Therefore, true solitude is not a mirror reflecting back the false self. Solitude fosters a communion with Christ within and consequently produces the fruits of love and compassion.

Merton repeats his admonition against that solitude of mere "interiorization" that can lead to narcissism. He emphasizes the importance of prayer, both vocal and contemplative, which requires a forgetfulness of the ego and all that is selfish. He also reminds us of the importance of reading, which draws us out of ourselves.

> Reading ought to be an act of homage to the God of all truth…. Reading gives God more glory when we get more out of it, when it is a more deeply vital act not only of our intelligence but of our whole personality, absorbed and refreshed in thought, meditation, prayer, or even in the contemplation of God.[9]

Thoughts in Solitude also contains Merton's most famous prayer which begins, "My Lord God, I have no idea where I am going." Merton asserts throughout the book that there is no need to know where one is going, for geography is of no importance in the inner life. You need only "rest in the being of God above your own being— Where your treasure is there your heart is also."[10]

Solitude was always important to Merton, even when he was a young monk. His abbot understood Merton's needs and realized that solitude was "medicine" for Merton. Before the Abbey's cinderblock hermitage was built, Merton gained access to an abandoned tool shed, daily using it as a kind of hermitage although he still lived within Gethsemani. *Thoughts in Solitude* was the fruit of Merton's solitary time spent in this rudimentary hermitage.

Bread in the Wilderness

For anyone unfamiliar with the Psalms, *Bread in the Wilderness* is an excellent introduction. Merton informs us that the Psalms are "perhaps the most significant and influential collection of religious poems ever written."[11] He compares the Psalms to bread: as bread nourishes the body so do the Psalms nourish the spirit. He says, "The Psalms acquire, for those who know how to enter into them, a surprising depth, a marvelous and inexhaustible actuality. They are bread, miraculously provided by Christ, to feed those who have followed Him into the wilderness."[12]

The Psalms are poems that lead the reader into the depths of the soul. They bring our minds and hearts into the presence of God. Praying the Psalms every day is part of the Church's life throughout the world. The beauty and the inspiration of these ancient prayer poems become our daily bread in the wilderness.

The Psalms, Merton reminds us, are not just poems: they are "religious poems" as opposed to devotional poems. Merton is careful to differentiate between religious and devotional poems: The latter are too often clichés of pious feelings, although composed with good intentions. The Psalms, on the other hand, are poems that spring from the depths of the soul where true religious experience abides. The Psalms were written, Merton tells us, by people who walked with God, by people for whom "God is above all things...and He is capable of manifesting Himself through them all."[13]

Meditation on the Psalms is a favored Christian practice because, Merton asserts, Christ's cross is the key to understanding the Psalms. Through the Psalms we "unite our sufferings with the sufferings of Christ."[14] From a Christian point of view, when the reader enters into the Psalms, he stands before Christ upon the Cross; he enters into his suffering; he becomes one with it. And in such union one is nourished as if by "bread in the wilderness."

Every page of *Bread in the Wilderness* gives us a glimpse of Merton the poet. A poet understands the lyric power of the Psalms as well as their mystery and sacredness. The Psalms are eloquent poems and prayers at the same time. In the Psalms, Merton discovered the reconciliation of his earlier conflict in believing poetry and contemplation antithetical. He saw in David, and the other psalmists, a mirror image of himself. They attempted to capture in words their seemingly ineffable experience of God, just as Merton undertook the same task in the twentieth century.

Merton encourages everyone to read the Psalms. They are not only for those who live a monastic life. He admits that the Psalms can be read as literature, as *poetry*, but he reminds us of the true author of the Psalms—the Holy Spirit who inspired the writers. When read with this understanding, the Psalms can "lead to contemplation precisely because their impact on us is *theological* rather than *psychological*."[15] In short, the Psalms lead us to God.

Merton the Poet

In his third book of poetry, *Figures for an Apocalypse*, Merton published the essay, "Poetry and the Contemplative Life," in its concluding pages. There, he wrestled with a dilemma: Are poetry and contemplation incompatible? In his own soul-searching he theorized that poetry may indeed be a serious obstacle to "actual sanctification" because it is world-oriented and subjective. But in time Merton would learn that his contemplative vocation did not exclude being faithful to his God-given poetic gifts. One can still love the world's beauty and remain an ascetic monk.

Like the monk, the poet is also marginal, one who is willing to embark on the interior journey in the search of self-knowledge; he or she is the sentry who exhorts us to look more attentively. The artist, Paul Klee, once said that, "Art does not reproduce what we see: it *makes* us see." Poetry *makes* us see.

During his own inner journey Merton discovered that Christ is our center and that Christ is the source of poetry. He wrote, "Christ is the inspiration of Christian poetry and Christ is at the center of the contemplative life."[16] And further:

Contemplation has much to offer poetry. And poetry, in its turn, has something to offer contemplation...the first thing that needs to be stressed is the essential dignity of the aesthetic experience. It is, in itself, a very high gift...it is a gift that very many people have never received, and which others, having received, have allowed to spoil or become atrophied within them through neglect and misuse.[17]

Merton came to understand that poetry was a necessary part of his continuing search for God, a search he faithfully chronicled in his verse. He felt compelled to record his experiences, but there is also a charitable dimension in verse-making. The poet is essentially altruistic because of the desire to share experiences. For many, Merton's poetry is not only a hosanna to God's ineffable beauty and love; it is also an exhortation to enter more deeply into the inner life.

Merton's verse extols silence and solitude, the *sine qua non* (without which, not) of the spiritual life. Perhaps one of his greatest contributions to modern life was his insistence on the necessity of silence and solitude in our lives. Only in silence and solitude are we able to cleanse the windows of our perception in order to see everything—God, the world and ourselves—anew. Merton, a man of faith in Christ, believed also in the higher calling of devoting oneself to poetry and art. He says, "the artist has the ability to penetrate not only the sensible surface of things but also into their inmost reality, even beyond to God himself."[18]

Poetry calls each of us to be a "new man." We are created anew each time we enter into a careful reading of a poem. Because words are sacred, they point to the holi-

ness of all God's creation: "Creatures can become, at t.
word of man, *sacred* signs and even sacraments. They can
acquire the power not only to manifest the might and
being of God by their own existence and their qualities,
but they can above all be signs of the infinite transcen-
dence of Him Who is Holy, and they can be symbols of
the hidden immanent action of the Holy One in His created universe."[19] Poetry attunes the soul to God because
it induces contact with the Creator of the universe.

Contemplation is spiritual wonder. Poetry is the fruit
of wonder. The poet's state of wonder, experienced vicariously by us as readers, possesses the potential to lift us
into a shared state of wonder. We forget ourselves when
we stand in humility and in awe before beauty. The artist's
moment of grace becomes ours.

We the Reader

Most of us are not monks, nor are we hermits. We
must live in a bustling world where there is often little
solitude or silence. But, to read poetry in a prayerful way,
it is useful to set aside some time of silence and solitude.
When we engage a poem, we must not be disturbed. Silence and solitude allow us to be captured by the beauty
within the poem, which pierces to the center of our be-

place where what Merton calls the true self
onating with the beauty of Christ within us.

calls us to be focused as we approach poetry.

to Czeslaw Milosz, a Nobel Prize winner for
..., Merton wrote:

What is happening in the world today is wholesale
collapse of man's capacity to love. He has been sub-
merged under material concerns, and by the fantastic
proliferation of men and things all around him, so
that there are so many of everything that one lives
in a state of constant bewilderment and fear. One
cannot begin to commit to any definite love, because
the whole game is too complex and too hazardous
and *one has lost all focus*. So we are carried away by
the whirlwind, and our children are even more
helpless than we ourselves.[20]

We cannot focus until we quiet ourselves and will
ourselves to pay attention. In fact, reading poetry is one
way to foster our ability to focus. Reading great religious
poetry is an experience of great dignity. We are made dig-
nified by our willingness to enter into the mind of the
poet who created the "word icon" of beauty.

To focus on a poem is to imitate the poet's attention
that initially brought the poem to birth, as D. H. Lawrence

wisely points out, a poem is an "act of attention."[21] Merton would agree with this definition of poetry. Attention's "long looking" can become contemplation that leads to "in-seeing" and insight.

Merton advises us to focus our attention upon the world, our neighbor and on God. To retrieve innocence and wonder, we need only surrender ourselves to the "seeds of contemplation" implanted, Merton reminds us, in all Christians at baptism.

> Contemplation is the highest expression of man's intellectual and spiritual life. It is that life itself, fully awake, fully active, and fully aware that it is alive. It is spiritual wonder. It is spontaneous awe at the sacredness of life, of being. It is gratitude for life, for awareness and for being. It is a vivid realization of the fact that life and being in us proceed from an invisible, transcendent and infinitely abundant Source.[22]

We all contain within us the beauty of the *Imago Dei* (Image of God). It is this beauty which attracts us to Beauty Itself, and makes us pursue it and attempt to recreate it. Thus, when we read poetry, we must approach it in humility. We must be willing to enter an unknown territory, a sacred ground that will allow us to be touched, astonished, and to again experience wonder. But to experience the light of beauty, we must cast aside all that is false, we must be stripped of all that is selfish.

> For Merton, the poet shares an analogous task, coaxing readers to recognize their illusory false self and creating the possibility of an alternative identity. For the monk, this ultimately led to [finding] the self in Christ. The poet recreates in images, symbols and metaphors such personifications of the inner self to awaken us.[23]

Practice as a Reader of Poetry

Let us look at one of Merton's early poems which will illustrate the kind of focusing that he encourages us to pursue.

The Reader

Lord, when the clock strikes
Telling the time with cold tin
And I sit hooded in this lectern

Waiting for the monks to come,
I see the red cheeses, and bowls
All smile with milk in ranks upon their tables.

Light fills my proper globe
(I have won light to read by
With a little, tinkling chain)

And the monks come down the cloister
With robes as voluble as water.
I do not see them but I hear their waves.

It is winter, and my hands prepare
To turn the pages of the saints:
And to the trees Thy moon has frozen on the windows
My tongue shall sing Thy Scripture.

Then the monks pause upon the step
(With me here in this lectern
And Thee there on Thy crucifix)
And gather little pearls of water on their fingers' ends
Smaller than this my psalm.

Notice that we have here a poem that is both a prayer
and a poem, beginning with the apostrophe "Lord." Thus,
a sacred reading of this poem is immediately called for.
Imagine Merton standing at the lectern in a balcony
above the tables of the monastic refectory. Customarily

Trappist monks eat in silence while listening to sacred reading, nourishing body and soul simultaneously.

While he waits for his brothers to assemble at their places at the tables, Merton sees red cheeses and bowls of milk. He sees all in the light of their simplicity and daily holiness, echoing Blake's "Everything that is / Is holy"— the kind of light he hopes will illuminate his mind and soul as his reading lamp illuminates the book before him.

Merton cannot see the monks arriving, but he hears them as "voluble as water." His hearing reaffirms his faith in those things unseen. He knows the monks will dip their fingers into the holy font before entering the refectory, a tradition dating back to medieval times when monks returning from the fields would stop to wash their hands before entering the dining room. He is ready to turn the holy page with his finger to allow "my tongue" to "sing Thy scripture"—his own symbolic cleansing.

In this poem, one not so much of reading as of vision, Merton, with rinsed eyes, sees his world with wonder. His monastic world itself becomes his sacred text, and as a poet he desires to capture this simple beauty before him; thus, beauty nourishes his creative spirit as the food on the tables nourishes the monks' bodies and the sacred text their souls. The utter simplicity of the poem demands a simple style of verse. "The Reader" is actually a breakthrough in Merton's poetic style with its austere verse line, which later culminates in what many consider one of his finest poems, "Elias—Variations on a Theme."

Merton describes the poem "The Reader" in the final verse, "Smaller than this my psalm." A psalm is a prayer (a lyrical poem) to the Lord; in fact, monks sing the whole Psalter (the collection of psalms) during their weekly prayer. Merton perceives no division between his poem and prayer; they become one. The paradigm is to be taken seriously: read poetry and become one with it so that it too becomes your prayer. Notice that in the last stanza Merton sees Christ, "there on Thy crucifix."

The incarnational dimension of the poem is again repeated with the monks dipping their fingers in holy water, a new baptism with the sign of the cross touching their body. The hands (representing the whole body) that work during the day are sacramentalized by holy water, as is Merton's hand by the turning of the sacred text: All the holy daily-ness of life is declared beautiful in Christ.

In "The Reader" Merton "reads" his world and by so doing he retrieves innocence. He shows us that the state of wonder can indeed be re-captured. Wonder is a natural state available not only to the poet but to all of us. In his *Letter to Artists* John Paul II says:

> On the threshold of the third millennium, my hope for all of you who are artists is that you will have an especially intense experience of creative inspiration. May the beauty which you pass on to generations still to come be such that it will *stir them to wonder!* Faced with the sacredness of life and of the human person, and before the marvels of the universe, wonder is the only appropriate attitude.[24]

Today, over thirty years after his death, Merton continues to inspire readers not only with the beauty of his spiritual classics, but also with the beauty of his poetry. He *stirs us to wonder*, reminding us that the gate to wonder is everywhere: Even at the lectern while waiting for his brothers to arrive for dinner.

CHAPTER 4

"Elias—Variations on a Theme"

I

Under the blunt pine
In the winter sun
The pathway dies
And the wilds begin.
Here the bird abides
Where the ground is warm
And sings alone.

Listen, Elias,
To the southern wind
Where the grass is brown,
Live beneath this pine
In wind and rain.
Listen to the woods,
Listen to the ground.

O listen, Elias
(Where the bird abides
And sings alone),
The sun grows pale
Where passes One
Who bends no blade, no fern.
Listen to His word.

> *"Where the fields end*
> *Thou shalt be My friend.*
> *Where the bird is gone*
> *Thou shalt be My son."*

How the pine burns
In the furious sun
When the prophets come
To Jerusalem.
(Listen, Elias,
To the fiery wing?)
To Jerusalem
Where the knife is drawn.

(Do her children run
To the covering wing?)

Look, look, My son,
At the smashed wood
At the bloody stone.

Where the fields end
And the stars begin
Listen, Elias,
To the winter rain.
For the seed sleeps
By the sleeping stone.
But the seed has life
While the stone has none.

> *"Where the fields end*
> *Thou shalt be My friend.*
> *Where the bird is gone*
> *Thou shalt be My son."*

II

There were supposed to be
Not birds but spirits of flame
Around the old wagon.
   ("Bring me my chariot")

There were supposed
To be fiery devices,
Grand machines, all flame,
With supernatural wings
Beyond the full creek.
("Bring me my chariot of fire")
All flame, beyond the rotten tree!
Flame? This old wagon
With the wet, smashed wheels
Is better. ("My chariot")
This derelict is better.
("Of fire.") It abides
(Swifter) in the brown ferns
And burns nothing. Bring me ("Of fire")
Better still the old trailer ("My chariot")
With the dead stove in it, and the rain
Comes down the pipe and covers the floor.
Bring me my chariot of rain. Bring me
My old chariot of broken-down rain.
Bring, bring my old fire, my old storm,
My old trailer; faster and faster it stands still,
Faster and faster it stays where it has always been,
Behind the felled oaks, faster, burning nothing.
Broken and perfect, facing south,

Facing the sound of distant guns,
Facing the wall of distance where blue hills
Hide in the fading rain.

Where the woods are cut down the punished
Trailer stands alone and becomes
(Against all the better intentions of the owners)
The House of God
The Gate of Heaven.
("My chariot of fire")

III

The seed, as I have said,
Hides in the frozen sod.
Stones, shaped by rivers they will
Never care about or feel,
Cover the cultivated soil.

The seed, by nature, waits to grow and bear
Fruit. Therefore it is not alone
As stones, or inanimate things are:
That is to say, alone by nature,
Or alone forever.

Where do so many waters come from on an empty hill?
Rain we had despaired of, rain
Which is sent from somewhere else, descended
To fix an exhausted mountain.
Listen to the waters, if possible,
And discern the words "False prophet"
False prophet! "So much better is the water's message,
So much more confident than our own. It is quite sure
You are a false prophet, so 'Go back'
(You have not had the patience of a rock or tree)
Go back into the cities. They want to receive you
Because you are not sent to them. You are a false prophet."

Go back where everyone, in heavy hours,
Is of a different mind, and each is his own burden,
And each mind is its own division
With sickness for diversion and war for
Business reasons. Go where the divided
Cannot stand to be too well. For then they would be
    held
Responsible for their own misery.

And I have been a man without silence,
A man without patience, with too many

Questions. I have blamed God
Thinking to blame only men
And defend Him Who does not need to be defended.
I have blamed ("defended") Him for Whom the wise
    stones
(Stones I lately condemned)
Waited in the patient
Creek that is now wet and clean of all ruins.

So now, if I were to return
to my own city (yes my own city), I would be
Neither accepted nor rejected.
For I have no message,
I would be lost together with the others.

IV

Under the blunt pine
I who am not sent
Remain. The pathway dies,
The journey has begun.
Here the bird abides
And sings on top of the forgotten
Storm. The ground is warm.

He sings no particular message.
His hymn has one pattern, no more planned,
No less perfectly planned
And no more arbitrary
Than the pattern in the seed, the salt,
The snow, the cell, the drop of rain.

(Snow says: I have my own pattern;
Rain says: no arbitrary plan!
River says: I go my own way.
Bird says: I am the same.
The pine tree says also:
Not compulsion plants me in my place,
No, not compulsion!)

The free man is not alone as busy men are
But as birds are. The free man sings
Alone as universes do. Built
Upon his own inscrutable pattern
Clear, unmistakable, not invented by himself alone
Or for himself, but for the universe also.

Nor does he make it his business to be recognized
Or care to have himself found out

As if some special subterfuge were needed
To get himself known for who he is.

The free man does not float
On the tides of his own expedition
Nor is he sent on ventures as busy men are,
Bound to an inexorable result:
But like the birds or lilies
He seeks first the Kingdom, without care.
Nor need the free man remember
Any street or city, or keep campaigns
In his head, or countries for that matter
Or any other economy.

                    Under the blunt pine
Elias becomes his own geography
(Supposing geography to be necessary at all),
Elias becomes his own wild bird, with God in the
    center,
His own wide field which nobody owns,
His own pattern, surrounding the Spirit
By which he is himself surrounded:

For the free man's road has neither beginning nor end.

CHAPTER 5

"Elias—Variations on a Theme": A Meditation

Critics have divided Merton's poetry into four groups: choir, desert, forest, and paradise. "Elias" falls into the desert category. As you pray this poem, notice the economy and austerity of the poetic line: its images are also stark: the "blunt pine" and "winter sun," the "winter rain" and the "sleeping stone." The geography is one of desert mystery, for there is no pathway to follow; it abruptly "dies."

As we have seen, poetry became Merton's locus where he found and defines himself, not only as a poet, but also as a man of spirit; "Elias—Variations on a Theme" represents the landscape of his soul. Its verses are "pathways" to the real journey, one that transcends the "geography" of stanza and verse: the inner journey.

For Merton, a successful inner journey requires a discarding of all that is extraneous. The stripped language of "Elias" corresponds to the stripping away of ego so that one's true self may be revealed. The setting of Merton's journey (and ours) implicitly warns us to cast off all that is superficial. The spiritual journey is one that purges all that is false, symbolized by a landscape where "the pine burns" and the sun is "furious." Merton writes, "The climate in which monastic prayer flowers is that of the desert, where the comfort of man is absent, where the secure routines of man's city offer no support, and where prayer must be sustained by God in the purity of faith."[1]

I

Under the blunt pine
In the winter sun
The pathway dies
And the wilds begin.
Here the bird abides
Where the ground is warm
And sings alone.

Now that I have visited Gethsemani and seen the red trailer under the huge pine tree where Thomas

Merton composed this poem, I understand more deeply his opening stanza. To find his trailer-hermitage, one must travel down a dirt path which leads into deeper woods and seemingly "dies." It is an area in which one could easily become lost.

We naturally ask ourselves why Merton would choose such a bleak landscape in which to live. In the early 1950s when Merton wrote "Elias" he had been searching for more solitude and silence in the monastic life. His fame as a spiritual writer had nearly destroyed his original purpose in entering the Abbey of Gethsemani: to disappear into God. Although the landscape appears to be bleak with a "winter sun" (the poem was written during the winter), and a "pathway" which "dies," and a place where the "wilds begin"; it is the site where Merton can "find" his soul. The bird is symbolic of the soul; the soul can indeed take flight in this stripped, wild land where the "ground is warm" and the bird "sings alone."

In Merton's vast poetic corpus, "Elias—Variations on a Theme" is the desert poem *par excellence*. Just as the ancients sequestered themselves in the desert for an uninterrupted, solitary encounter with God, so too Merton has entered the woods of Kentucky—the closest alternative to a desert experience for an American Trappist monk. Such an exterior landscape is a prompt for a Trappist—in emulation of the bare desert, he prays to be stripped of all that is not of God. His only visible companions are of nature: the blunt pine, the winter sun, the dying pathway and the solitary bird. All these desert images suggest the purgative stage of the mystical journey.

At first the natural setting appears to be hostile and unappealing, but Merton says the "ground is warm." The ground is warm from the sun, but it is also warm because the earth is hospitable and inviting; it is mother earth. Merton's love of nature reminds us that he had read Thoreau and admired this poet who chose to live alone at the edge of Walden Pond. In his own way, Merton lives a Thoreauvian life. The difference between the austere New Englander and the Trappist is that Merton does not seek a vague transcendental communion with nature, but mystical union with God.

Listen, Elias,
To the southern wind
Where the grass is brown,
Live beneath this pine
In wind and rain.
Listen to the woods,
Listen to the ground.

O listen, Elias
(Where the bird abides
And sings alone),
The sun grows pale
Where passes One
Who bends no blade, no fern.
Listen to His word.

Here we are first introduced to the Elias *persona* (Latin for *mask*). Merton imagines himself as Elias. Elias is Elijah, an Old Testament prophet of the northern kingdom during the reign of King Ahab. He had been sent by God to chastise Ahab for encouraging the worship of Baal, a pagan god of storm and rain. In the midst of a three-year famine, God commands the despairing Elijah to depart and live by himself. Elijah stations himself under a juniper tree near water; God commands the ravens to provide him with daily bread.

Later, Elijah finds his way to Mount Horeb where he spends the night in a cave. He attentively listens for God's voice until God reveals himself, not in powerful thunder or lightning, but in a gentle, barely audible breeze. Elijah's life, therefore, is symbolic of the contemplative life of waiting and listening.

Merton's command to himself via Elias is to listen.

Later we shall see why Merton repeats this command throughout the poem. Merton became a monk to listen to the word of God in silence and solitude. His daily life, however, became caught up in matters he could not have predicted: he became an international best-selling author; the demand for more books grew and Merton surrendered himself to producing them at a fast pace. He was also pursued by scores of people: ordinary folk seeking spiritual counsel, people with personal problems, intellectuals seeking dialogue, the famous trying to touch base with another renowned figure. Innumerable requests poured into Gethsemani and Merton's time for listening to the word of God drastically diminished. To please his abbot and satisfy his own needs as a writer, he succumbed to the demands.

His inner self, however, quietly reminded the young "prophet" to listen. But listen to what? God doesn't speak directly to many people, unless one is a visionary like Elijah. Listen to what? Listen to the "southern wind" and the "wind and rain" and the "woods" and the "ground." Listen to God's creation, for it is a model for all of us to follow. Nature "naturally" performs the will of God. The wind blows, the rain pours, the bird sings, the sun grows pale and even the ground follows its calling—it is warm.

Elias, an alias for Merton, must follow his vocation—he must listen for the word of God. He must do so carefully, because God rarely leaves obvious signs of his presence: He "bends no blade, no fern." Elias looks, but sees nothing, because a breeze is not visible but audible. Prayer, therefore, is exquisite hearing—listening to the still, small voice.

> *"Where the fields end*
> *Thou shalt be My friend.*
> *Where the bird is gone*
> *Thou shalt be My son."*

This refrain is placed within quotation marks to denote God's voice, promising that in our listening we become God's children. We move from mere friendship with God in these lines to being his sons and daughters.

How the pine burns
In the furious sun
When the prophets come
To Jerusalem.
(Listen, Elias,
To the fiery wing?)
To Jerusalem
Where the knife is drawn.

The sun is "furious," symbolic of purgation. The Desert Fathers went to the desert to fast and to pray in imitation of John the Baptist and Jesus Christ. This was a harshly ascetic life lived where the sun burned away all that interfered with the relationship with God. Symbolically, it burned away sin and cleansed the soul, making it more worthy of God's presence. Perhaps here Merton is also "furious," angered by his own false worship of fame, his failure to follow more fully his contemplative vocation.

(Do her children run
To the covering wing?)
Look, look, My son,
At the smashed wood
At the bloody stone.

Elijah gathered Ahab and the false prophets of Baal at Mount Carmel to prove the identity of the true God. He commanded that two altars be built for the sacrifice of two bulls. The Baalan prophets called upon their god to send down fire to consume their offering. Nothing happened. Elijah built his altar of wood and stone and placed on it the bull, drenching everything in water to prove God's power. He then called upon God to answer him. The fire of the Lord fell and consumed the offering along with the wood and the stones and the dust and it licked up all the water (cf. 1 Kgs 18:1–40).

Merton has no need to prove the identity of God. He has no need to prove which prophets are the true prophets. He is not called upon to set fire to an offering. But he is called to be an offering—to sacrifice his own self for God. Such an offering is the core of his monastic vocation—to sacrifice the ego for the love of God. The ego is to be burned away by the "furious sun." The sun is relentless because so much of Merton's false ego remains intact despite the desert landscape.

Where the fields end
And the stars begin
Listen, Elias,
To the winter rain.
For the seed sleeps
By the sleeping stone.
But the seed has life
While the stone has none.

Merton doesn't know where the "fields end." He doesn't know where the "stars begin." Such geographical knowledge is unnecessary in the pursuit of God, for to know where the field ends and the stars begin is to know the whole journey. Such knowledge is not available in temporal time—only in eternity.

To pursue God, Merton need only "Listen." The "seed sleeps" brings to mind the symbolic potential we all possess to listen to the voice of God. The "winter rain" will nourish the seed, but the seed's fruition depends on how much of the life-giving water it absorbs. So, like Merton, we must also listen; the more we listen, the better able we are to absorb the life-giving word of God. And of course, listening is an act of the will. People can listen, but they can also choose to be "stone" deaf.

"Where the fields end
Thou shalt be My friend.
Where the bird is gone
Thou shalt be My son."

Again we are reminded that the reward of listening is to know oneself as God's friend, and finally as God's child.

What is the primary practice of desert spirituality? It is the act of listening. Jonathan Montaldo, a Merton critic, emphasizes Merton's spirituality of vigilant listening:

The spiritual practice flowing through Merton's journals like an underground stream is an attentive, faithful, and sober listening. His path toward human wisdom was an ancient one: Merton was Benedictine to the bone. The first counsel of St. Benedict of Nursia's Rule for Monks is "Listen, listen very carefully, child, to the words of the Master".... This culture of listening permeates Merton's autobiographical writing and witnesses to his traditionally monastic spirit.[2]

And to what should we listen? Merton suggests everything: the wind, the rain, the woods, and even the ground—perhaps the "ground of our being." Why? Because God is omnipresent. And if we are to become aware of God's presence, we must go where the "bird abides." The bird also symbolizes the voice of God. Yet the bird is swift, it hides and "sings alone"; thus, the only way to locate the bird is to develop an ear for exquisite listening. One must "Listen to his word" spoken by the "still, small voice" (cf. 1 Kgs 19:12).

Merton's poem "Elias" is perhaps a response to several of T. S. Eliot's poems, specifically the "Four Quartets" and "The Hollow Men," also a desert poem. In "The Hollow Men," Eliot writes:

This is the dead land
This is the cactus land
Here the stone images

Are raised, here they receive
The supplication of a dead man's hand
Under the twinkle of a fading star.

The difference between Merton and Eliot's poems is that Merton is a man of faith and hope whereas Eliot (before his Christian conversion) was a man of despair, his faith nothing but "the twinkle of a fading star." Thus, for Eliot the desert is a place of darkness and death. For Merton, however, the desert is a place of purification, of diminishment, of stripping, of *kenosis* (emptying), of silence, of solitude.... The desert becomes the locus, not of a deadened landscape, but of a *soul-scape* where there can be a real encounter with the Divine. Commenting on Merton, George Kilcourse writes:

> Merton always nudges us toward solitude and the interior desert to confront our poverty and to renounce the empirical self. Then our encounter with "emptiness" flowers in the birth and awakening of the true self, the very self who "imitates Christ."[3]

II

Variation II addresses the biblical story of the prophet Elias's (Elijah) being taken up to heaven in a chariot of fire.

There were supposed to be
Not birds but spirits of flame
Around the old wagon.
("Bring me my chariot")
There were supposed
To be fiery devices,
Grand machines, all flame,
With supernatural wings
Beyond the full creek.

Merton's own chariot of fire is not one surrounded by "spirits of flame." There are no "supernatural wings" here—just the wings of local birds. Nothing like "grand machines." Just an ordinary red trailer.

But for Merton an ordinary red trailer is sufficient. For Merton much depends on his red trailer: true, it is not Elias's fiery chariot, but it is the primary place for Merton to pursue silence, to pursue solitude, to write poetry, and ultimately, to commune with God. Nothing extraordinary is needed—simply a place to sit, to wait and to listen.

("Bring me my chariot of fire")
All flame, beyond the rotten tree!
Flame? This old wagon

With the wet, smashed wheels
Is better. ("My chariot")
This derelict is better.
("Of fire.") It abides
(Swifter) in the brown ferns
And burns nothing.

Merton prefers the "old wagon / With the wet, smashed wheels." His humility requires nothing to boost his ego. He is not Elias, he isn't a prophet, he doesn't need a chariot: "This derelict is better" because it abides, not in the sky, but humbly in the "brown ferns."

The theme of this variation of "Elias" is one Merton reiterates later: I, the writer and the monk Thomas Merton, am not a prophet. Merton needs not a "chariot of fire" but an "old trailer / With the dead stove in it." So there will be no miraculously inflamed, flying chariot, only a "derelict" trailer that moves nowhere, but stays "Behind the felled oaks, faster, burning nothing." The setting of "felled oaks" is the one preferred by the fallen man, who here is Merton, the monk and poet. By rejecting ostentation (a fiery chariot) to embrace humility (a derelict shed) and preferring "wet, smashed wheels" over "supernatural wings," Merton affirms who he is: a contemplative

Trappist monk. The red trailer, therefore, symbolizes the kind of person Merton is before God: a humble, imperfect, man.

Bring me ("Of fire")
Better still the old trailer ("My chariot")
With the dead stove in it, and the rain
Comes down the pipe and covers the floor.
Bring me my chariot of rain. Bring me
My old chariot of broken-down rain.
Bring, bring my old fire, my old storm,
My old trailer; faster and faster it stands still,
Faster and faster it stays where it has always been,
Behind the felled oaks, faster, burning nothing.

Merton's red trailer is soaked in rain water as "the rains come down the pipe and covers the floor." The rain symbolizes purification, baptism, transformation, in short, the "old trailer" is Merton's place of rebirth; it is "The House of God / The Gate of Heaven." The trailer is what will suffice for Merton. There is no need now for him to travel anywhere beyond his own hermitage.

In a larger sense the trailer could be likened to the Abbey of Gethsemani where Merton renounced all to become a humble monk. In the enclosure of the abbey,

Merton devotes his life to burning away all that is false—
by the fire of purification, of asceticism, and of prayer.

III

The seed, as I have said,
Hides in the frozen sod.
Stones, shaped by rivers they will
Never care about or feel,
Cover the cultivated soil.

The seed, by nature, waits to grow and bear
Fruit. Therefore it is not alone
As stones, or inanimate things are:
That is to say, alone by nature,
Or alone forever.

Early in his monastic and poetic career the symbol
of seeds became rooted in Merton's mind. In the opening paragraph of his first book on spiritual direction,
Merton says:

> Every moment and every event of man's life on earth
> plants something in his soul. For just as the wind
> carries thousands of invisible and visible winged
> seeds, so the stream of time brings with it germs of

spiritual vitality that come to rest imperceptibly in the minds and wills of men. Most of these unnumbered seeds perish and are lost, because men are not prepared to receive them: for such seeds as these can not spring up anywhere except in the good soil of liberty and desire.[4]

Here the seed represents the inner life with its inner center where the true self can be encountered. The seed symbolizes the potential every Christian possesses to touch and be touched by the Divine. The seed "hides"; it grows in secret; it is nurtured by contemplation, perhaps "seeds of contemplation." The seed has the potential to grow and flower into fruit. It is unlike the lifeless stone that covers the earth. Stones are "inanimate things." They are also solitary; they contain within them no seed that will someday grow. They remain "alone forever."

If we as Christians are asked to choose between being seeds and stones, we surely know our answer. We recall Christ's parable of the mustard seed (cf. Mk 4:30–34). We also recall the incident of the woman caught in adultery and the men who were about to stone her (cf. Jn 8:1–11). When Christ said, "He who is without sin cast the first stone," each man dropped his stone and departed. Surely Merton had both of these Gospel passages in mind.

The seed "waits to grow and bear / Fruit." This is another New Testament reference, to "a tree known by its fruit" (Lk 6: 41–43). The seed must be patient, it waits, grows, and finally bears fruit. The spiritual life has its own holy rhythm and maturation.

In these two stanzas, Merton stresses the spiritual way of waiting. Waiting also implies listening. Only by waiting and listening to the "still, small voice" will we grow and mature as Christians. But we must do our waiting and listening in a certain spirit: we must *care*. To care suggests involvement, nurturing attention—all of which is done preferably in silent secrecy. The seed hides in the ground, to burst through the earth later, make known its presence, and offer its fruit.

If we follow this paradigm of spirituality, we pray and praise God in secret. Not that we do not participate in public prayer, we come together to celebrate the Eucharist daily or weekly. As Christians we must sometimes take a public stand. But we remember Christ's encouragement to pray privately to the Father as well.

We find in Merton's essay "Philosophy of Solitude" a description of the kind of man he hoped to become. In this essay, written at approximately the time as "Elias," Merton says:

The emptiness of the true solitary is marked then by a great simplicity. This simplicity can be deceptive, because it may be hidden under a surface of apparent complexity, but it is there nevertheless, behind the outer contradictions of the man's life. It manifests itself in a kind of candor though he may be very reticent. There is in this lonely one a gentleness, a deep sympathy, though he may be apparently antisocial. There is a great purity of love, though he may hesitate to manifest his love in any way, or to commit himself openly to it.[5]

Where do so many waters come from on an empty hill?
Rain we had despaired of, rain
Which is sent from somewhere else, descended
To fix an exhausted mountain.
Listen to the waters, if possible,
And discern the words "False prophet"
False prophet! "So much better is the
water's message,
So much more confident than our own.
It is quite sure
You are a false prophet, so 'Go back'
(You have not had the patience of a rock or tree)

Go back into the cities. They want to receive you
Because you are not sent to them. You are a false
prophet."

The above verses address the themes of emptiness, despair, and exhaustion. Rain, symbolic of God's mercy, arrives "to fix" the "exhausted mountain." (Here, we cannot help but think of Merton as the "exhausted mountain" of *The Seven Storey Mountain.* Having grown so much spiritually, did Merton see himself as having once been a false prophet in his autobiography?) The rain refreshes and renews because it knows what is false and what is true. Here, the full weight of his calling as monk and poet seems to weigh upon Merton. Again he chides himself for not having the "patience of a rock or tree," for not listening. If he had listened more attentively, perhaps he might not have been trapped in the "persona of the prophet." False prophets have their own cities where "They want to receive you / Because you are not sent to them."

But, as with all good things, rain comes from God. Rain arrives as does grace in our spiritual lives. Fortunately, for all of us, it "descends" to refresh and renew us when we are truly exhausted or most arid spiritually.

Go back where everyone, in heavy hours,
Is of a different mind, and each is his own burden,
And each mind is its own division
With sickness for diversion and war for
Business reasons. Go where the divided
Cannot stand to be too well. For then they would be
  held
Responsible for their own misery.

This is a description of a post-World War II society trapped in a new form of combat: the Cold War—a place with "its own division," of "diversion and war," of "misery"; a place where people "cannot stand to be too well." This is the place for false prophets and for persons who choose their own anguish. In such a place, the false prophet feels at home. This is a place where people blame their unhappiness on others.

Although sequestered in a monastery, Merton confesses to being a part of this modern world; he chastises himself for being unfaithful to his ideal of a hidden life, saying:

And I have been a man without silence,
A man without patience, with too many
Questions. I have blamed God

Thinking to blame only men
And defend Him Who does not need to be defended.
I have blamed ("defended") Him for Whom the wise
    stones
(Stones I lately condemned)
Waited in the patient
Creek that is now wet and clean of all ruins.

Here Merton totally divests himself of Elias's prophetic persona. We see the naked Merton, the monk and poet looking at himself directly and not liking what he sees. It takes courage and blunt, if not brutal, honesty to face one's false self in the interior mirror of the true self. Again, Merton perceives that he has been this "man without silence."

Merton also accuses himself of not being "patient." He always felt the temptation to seek more solitude and silence, not at his own abbey but elsewhere…the West Coast, Mexico, Alaska, Latin America…. His abbot often counseled Merton to be patient and wait upon the Lord, to consider thoughts of leaving Gethsemani as a temptation; sound advice which Merton, perhaps not always gracefully, followed.

Merton's "blaming" is certainly a reference to his earlier judgmental tendency. Of course, he now recognizes that throwing stones at others is not Christ-like. It accomplishes nothing. In both his autobiography, and the first edition of *Seeds of Contemplation*, Merton projected much of his own shadow (the negative aspects of his personality) onto society, seeing "the world" as dangerous and evil. He gradually learned that all people, whether within or without the abbey, are not very different, and that everyone requires God's love and mercy.

Throughout "Elias," Merton tries to keep his feet on the ground. No ascending chariots for him. But keeping his ego grounded required a constant examination of conscience that found its way into his poetry and journals. In an unpublished paper, Jonathan Montaldo, a Merton authority, refers to several journal entries where Merton chastises himself for his ego-inflation. Merton realized that he deeply craved the admiration of others. He wanted to be, as he said, "the one, original cloistered genius, the tonsured wonder of the Western world."[6] In another entry, Merton accuses himself of arrogance, "Someone accused me of being a 'high priest' of creativity. Or at least of allowing people to regard me as one. This is perhaps true.... The sin of *wanting to be a pontiff* [Merton's emphasis], of wanting to be heard, of wanting converts, disciples.... I have got to face the fact that there is in me a desire for survival as pontiff, prophet, and writer, and this has to be renounced before I can be myself at last."[7]

And so, composing poetry is sacramental for Merton. His verse became the confessional where he recorded his failures in the hope that such confessions would lead him toward self-knowledge and a deeper understanding of his inner journey.

So now, if I were to return
to my own city (yes my own city), I would be
Neither accepted nor rejected.
For I have no message,
I would be lost together with the others.

What city is Merton referring to? Cosmopolitan London? To Cambridge where, as an undergraduate, he was a libertine? To New York and Columbia University where he finally turned to the Church? And is he better off than the inhabitants of these cities? Merton says no. He feels that he has not achieved sainthood; he is not even a modern prophet. He is still the "broken" Merton seeking God's perfection while "facing the sound of distant guns."

IV

In the fourth variation, Merton continues his abandonment of the Elias persona and reveals himself, unmediated except by language—a stark, clean, and precise language.

Under the blunt pine
I who am not sent
Remain. The pathway dies,
The journey has begun.

Merton is alone under a pine tree, alone because the inner journey is a solitary one. Merton has already stripped himself of one false self: "I who am not sent." At this point, he feels he is not a God-sent prophet like Elias, just an ordinary man. The "pathway dies" because every person's journey is singular: there is no path which others have trod that he can follow. He will "Remain" because there is nowhere externally to go; the real journey is within.

The "blunt pine" suggests the "tree of knowledge" in the Garden of Eden; it also calls to mind the tree of the cross of Christ, "the Wisdom of God and the Power of God" (1 Cor 1:24). The appearance of trees as an image, according to Carl Jung, is often symbolic of the general archetype of transformation; they suggest rooted-ness, repose, growth, and fruition, as well as a union of earth and sky.

Here the bird abides
And sings on top of the forgotten
Storm. The ground is warm.
He sings no particular message.
His hymn has one pattern, no more planned,
No less perfectly planned
And no more arbitrary
Than the pattern in the seed, the salt,
The snow, the cell, the drop of rain.

Merton's imagery suggests that embarking on the inner journey requires one to be humble, small—like the seed, the grain of salt, the evanescent snow, the microscopic cell, the fragile drop of rain. It is necessary to know one's own nothingness. Merton's verse echoes T. S. Eliot's "Four Quartets": "The only wisdom we can hope to acquire / Is the wisdom of humility, humility is endless."

As with nature's humble diminutives, one's own pattern offers no "particular message." One listens to the bird, symbolic of the "still, small voice" of God.

The free man is not alone as busy men are

But as birds are. The free man sings
Alone as universes do. Built
Upon his own inscrutable pattern
Clear, unmistakable, not invented by himself alone
Or for himself, but for the universe also.

A "free man" is not as "busy men," getting and spending. He sings "Alone as universes do." He is poetically one with the universe; he is an integrated man. Here, we think of the harmony of the spheres, the music created by the planets because, following their individual patterns, they are in communion with each other around the sun. Harmony is "Built." This implies that harmony is the result of conscious consent and a will responding to Christ's will. The freedom and harmony of wholeness is "clear, unmistakable" when it is achieved. And this wholeness reaches out to others, to the universe.

The free man does not float
On the tides of his own expedition
Nor is he sent on ventures as busy men are,
Bound to an inexorable result:
But like the birds or lilies
He seeks first the Kingdom, without care.
Nor need the free man remember

Any street or city, or keep campaigns
In his head, or countries for that matter
Or any other economy.

    Merton reinforces the symbolic significance of a journey without geography—it is beyond place; yet is found in the individual soul. The "free man" is "like the birds or lilies / He seeks first the Kingdom, without care." Immediately Christ's sayings, "consider the lilies of the field" (Mt 6:28) and, "the kingdom of heaven is within you" (Lk 17:21) come to mind. Christ's reference to the lilies of the field was his word of advice to us on how to face anxiety. Worrying or fixating on the future solves nothing. As Dante counseled in *The Divine Comedy*—*la sua voluntade è nostra pace*—"His will is our peace." We also recall Eliot's verse from "Ash Wednesday": "Teach us not to care." We should not care more about the things of the world than about matters of the spirit.

                 Under the blunt pine
Elias becomes his own geography
(Supposing geography to be necessary at all),
Elias becomes his own wild bird, with God in the
    center,

His own wide field which nobody owns,
His own pattern, surrounding the Spirit
By which he is himself surrounded:

This last stanza describes a person who has discovered his true self "under the blunt pine." "Blunt" suggests honesty; a person must be honest with himself in order to achieve spiritual integration, a union with Christ that comes from following "His own pattern." To become whole (holy) he must win "his wide field," an increased awareness of his true center in Christ: "with God in the Center." Thus the "wide field" corresponds to an enlightened soul, one expanded and centered in God, a person of psychic and spiritual wholeness.

We might ask why Merton uses the metaphor "geography." Perhaps he is suggesting that a free man needs neither "street," "city," nor "country." Perhaps Merton chides himself for his insistence on having a private hermitage. In the end, as he suggests, the place or geography are of least importance since those who are free need only enter themselves to discover the Alpha and the Omega.

The final verse of "Elias" is separated from the rest of the poem for emphasis:

For the free man's road has neither beginning nor end.

The free person's road *is* God; God, who is the Alpha and the Omega; God without beginning or end.

Was Merton a truly free person when he composed "Elias" in 1954–1955? From his own words we can only know that he was a person intent upon the spiritual journey, devoted to the search for a deeper life centered upon Christ. In "Elias," Merton the poet had finally achieved verse both sharp and precise, verse of fire with an intense heat, not of excoriation, but of exhortation. He echoes Saint Paul in urging us to find within ourselves the Christ who is our Center: "Not I, but Christ lives in me" (cf. Gal 2:20).

After praying a poem such as "Elias," we are inspired to transform our lives, to simplify, to reduce life to what is most essential. In short, we desire holiness. Merton had no illusions about how difficult it is to become holy. It was difficult for the early Desert Fathers and it is still difficult for us today; but holiness is, indeed, available to everyone. Merton encourages us in this vein, "The spiritual life is not a life of quiet withdrawal, a hot house growth of artificial ascetic practices beyond the reach of people living ordinary lives. It is in the ordinary duties and labors of life that the Christian can and should develop his spiritual union with God."[8]

Merton also realized that holiness is not so much a pursuit of perfection as a pursuit of wholeness. He says that if we are to be "perfect," we must be more human, not less human. He says sanctity "implies a greater concern for suffering, for understanding, for sympathy, and also for humor, for joy, for appreciation of the good and beautiful things of life."[9]

Merton realized, just as the Desert Fathers Cassian and Jerome had, that we can only be "*relatively* perfect in the present life."[10] We devote our efforts, on a daily basis, to stripping away what is false in our lives. But we cannot forget that a holy life is founded on Christ's love, and that every Christian has access to hidden fountains of divine grace, which he or she can drink from at every moment of life.

What kind of man had Merton become after twenty-seven years in a Trappist monastery? Merton reveals this in his own words:

> The grip the present has on me. That is the one thing that has grown most noticeably in the spiritual life—nothing much else has. The rest dims as

it should. I am getting older. The reality of now—the unreality of all the rest. The unreality of ideas and explanations and formulas. I am. The unreality of all the rest. The pigs shriek. Butterflies dance together—or danced together a moment ago—against the blue sky at the end of the woodshed. The buzz saw stands outside there, half covered with dirty and tattered canvas. The trees are fresh and green in the sun (more rain yesterday). Small clouds in-expressibly beautiful and silent and eloquent, over the silent woodlands. What a celebration of light, quietness and glory! This is my feast, sitting here in the straw.[11]

If prayer is attention, then here we see Merton in ecstatic prayer. Here he is in union with Reality. Here he is serene and happy, glorifying God's "Now moment," attentive to all that is before him. Surely such attentive, appreciative living is something to be hoped for in our lives.

At the end of his life the great mystical scholar Saint Thomas Aquinas said that his *Summa Theologica* was so much straw to be burned. And here we have Merton abiding in the sacramental Holy Now, transmuting straw (as if from the manger) into a holy, golden cushion upon which he sits under the blunt pine "with God in the center" of all his life—Now. We are all summoned to such a "feast."

CHAPTER 6

"Night-Flowering Cactus"

I know my time, which is obscure, silent and brief
For I am present without warning one night only.

When the sun rises on the brass valleys I become
   serpent.

Though I show my true self only in the dark and to
   no man
(For I appear by day as serpent)
I belong neither to night nor day.

Sun and city never see my deep white bell
Or know my timeless moment of void:
There is no reply to my munificence.

When I come I lift my sudden Eucharist
Out of the earth's unfathomable joy

Clean and total I obey the world's body
I am intricate and whole, not art but wrought passion
Excellent deep pleasure of essential waters
Holiness of form and mineral mirth:

I am the extreme purity of virginal thirst.

I neither show my truth nor conceal it
My innocence is descried dimly
Only by divine gift
As a white cavern without explanation.

He who sees my purity
Dares not speak of it.
When I open once for all my impeccable bell
No one questions my silence:
The all-knowing bird of night flies out of my mouth.

Have you seen it? Then though my mirth has
    quickly ended
You live forever in its echo:
You will never be the same again.

CHAPTER 7

"Night-Flowering Cactus": A Meditation

In "Elias—Variations on a Theme" Merton hides behind the persona of the prophet Elijah, doffing this likeness only at intervals. In "Night-Flowering Cactus," however, the poet becomes one with the object of his gaze, totally submerging himself in the symbolism. Merton perceives himself as the cactus; for him the cactus represents both the person he is and his way of life. Merton's friend Robert Lax went so far as to say that "Night-Flowering Cactus" served as Merton's spiritual autobiography[1]; thus, "Night-Flowering Cactus" is revelatory not only of Merton's contemplative vocation, but also of his personality.

From a theological perspective "Night-Flowering Cactus" recalls the mystical way known as the *via negativa* (negative way). This is the spiritual way of Saint John of the Cross, the mystic whom Merton most loved and tried to emulate as a young monk, the spiritual master he never abandoned. Merton embraced this *via negativa* because it suited him both temperamentally and intellectually. He was a solitary and introspective man who understood that God cannot be completely defined by the intellect and the *via negativa* also appealed to his sense of stark asceticism.

I know my time, which is obscure, silent and brief
For I am present without warning one night only.

It is surprising to find a poem beginning with the personal pronoun "I" when the theme of the poem addresses the "disappearance of the "I" into God. But in order for Merton to dramatize the beauty of the contemplative life, he must personify the "Night-Flowering Cactus" by permitting it to speak its own soliloquy. The night-flowering cactus humbly admits the extent of its knowledge: "I know my time." This resonates not only with knowledge of time itself, but with knowledge of the world in which one lives. Merton also understood his time—he knew his generation, its ailments and, finally, he believed the cure for modern society's woes lay in following God's will. After becoming a Trappist, Merton's *raison d'être*, his reason for being, was to know himself through God and to follow God's will.

During the day, the night-flowering cactus reveals only its thorny self to the world. And Merton, with his high ideals, remained human. He could be thorny with both his fellow brothers and with his abbot, and he was sometimes quite curt with his manuscript secretaries when they couldn't read his handwriting. In some ways he was a restless man in search of peace; the noise about the monastery—the farming tractors as well as the gunfire that could be heard coming from the nearby Fort Knox—grated harshly on his silence-seeking personality.

Despite its thorns, the night-flowering cactus knows its time. It knows when to bloom and when to reveal its treasure. Its manifestation is at night when all is obscure and silent; its flowering is "present without warning one night only."

In these two verses of stunning economy, Merton presents a whole way of life. It is the way of life he has chosen for himself. He, too, lives in the "desert" obscurity of the Abbey of Gethsemani, hidden in the hill country of Kentucky far from cities. His life, too, is silent as he waits upon the Lord, who, like the night-flowering cactus, appears "without warning." In fact, Merton's life is one of total attention on the hoped-for signs of the presence of the Divine. Being a contemplative, Merton knows that such glimpses beyond the veil, if granted, are ever so "sudden" and "brief."

The "cover" of the night is characteristic of the spiritual way embraced by such mystics as the anonymous author of the *Cloud of Unknowing*, the early Christian mystic Pseudo-Dionysius, and the Desert Fathers who sought God in the loneliness, silence and obscurity of the wilderness.

Merton prays in obscurity and in silence. A letter from Merton to the Sufi mystic, Abdul Aziz, is of particular interest because it is the only time he describes his own personal practice of prayer.

> I have a very simple way of prayer. It is centered entirely on attention to the presence of God and to His will and His love.... One might say this gives my meditation the character described by the Prophet as "being before God as if you saw Him." Yet it does not mean imagining anything or conceiving a precise image of God, for to my mind this would be a kind of idolatry.[2]

Our God is often a hidden God. But there are times when He is present to us, when He comes "without warning" and all we can do as Christians is to be attentive.

When the sun rises on the brass valleys I become
   serpent.

"I become serpent." The image of a serpent is often seen as a pejorative one, but perhaps here it has a positive connotation, such as Christ's warning for us to live in this world as persons who are as gentle as doves and as wise as serpents (cf. Mt 10:16). Living in the sun is a challenge akin to living in a world where it is unwise to reveal our vulnerability to anyone and everyone. We learn at an early age to don a persona and, from a psychological perspective, such a mask is at times necessary; it helps to protect and preserve us from being wounded. Similarly, the thorny exterior of the cactus protects and guards its precious inner treasure.

Though I show my true self only in the dark and to
   no man
(For I appear by day as serpent)
I belong neither to night nor day.

The bloom here is symbolic of the spiritual beauty of the "true self" which is rooted in God. Merton describes this true self:

At the center of our being is a point of nothingness

which is untouched by sin and by illusion, a point of pure truth, a point or spark which belongs entirely to God, which is never at our disposal, from which God disposes of our lives, which is inaccessible to the fantasies of our own mind or the brutalities of our own will. This little point of nothingness and of absolute poverty is the pure glory of God in us.... It is in everybody...I have no program for this seeing. It is only given. But the gate of heaven is everywhere.[3]

Merton's poetic verse corresponds with his prosaic account of God touching the soul. We never know when or how God will reveal himself. Merton cannot offer any guide or "program for this seeing." Like the night-flowering cactus, God comes when he comes; his epiphany, this revealing himself to us, is a perpetual possibility.

The flower belongs "neither to night nor day." Beauty of nature and soul belongs to God alone. God is Beauty and abides neither in day nor in night, but in the eternal Now. Sometimes we are gifted with a "timeless moment." When we are allowed a glimpse beyond the veil, we experience an epiphanic moment in our lives. Such events are chronicled by mystics, poets and saints, but are available to us all. Through prayer and through the experience of beauty, we maintain our contact with God, and so leave ourselves open to his grace-full touch.

The secret flower of the cactus correlates with the secret of our identity, which Merton says is "hidden in the love and mercy of God."[4] He further states that the only way "I can be myself is to become identified with him in Whom is hidden the reason and fulfillment of my existence."[5] Finally, the true self is discovered when God is discovered: "If I find him, I will find myself and if I find my true self I will find him."[6]

Reading poetry is a way of self-discovery that in turn can lead us to God. Poems like the "Night-Flowering Cactus" reveal their beauty in obscurity and silence. We have to look carefully, to read closely and silently in order to approach the poem's mystery whose meaning is often obscured by difficult images and esoteric symbols.

For a moment, imagine Merton going out into the night in search of the night-flowering cactus. By searching he makes an act of faith, for he believes in the object of his quest. He must then locate it and patiently wait for its unfolding loveliness. Searching and waiting—is not this the way of all mystics?

Sun and city never see my deep white bell
Or know my timeless moment of void:
There is no reply to my munificence.

The inner flower lives a hidden life far away from the prying eyes of bustling cities and even from the eye of the firmament, the sun. Merton always distrusted city life; he saw it with its noise, overcrowding and materialism as a place antithetical to the contemplative life.

The bloom is compared to a "deep white bell." Such a metaphor is appropriate because Merton's life revolved around the abbey bells which announced the Liturgical Hours throughout the day. And there were also the bells during the daily Eucharist, proclaiming the presence of Christ at the moment of consecration. When Merton moved to his hermitage, he was still close enough to the abbey to hear its bells—a constant reminder that a monk's life centers, first and foremost, around prayer.

But here the night-flowering cactus announces its beauty in the darkness of the night simply by being. No sound emanates from its "timeless moment of void." This calls forth God's appearance in our lives; his silent announcement is known, his presence irradiates our being. We must be empty, a void, so to speak, in order to be filled by God's radiance, unfolding in the timelessness of eternity.

The concept of the *void* was one that intrigued Merton in his study of Zen Buddhism. For the Buddhist, the void is a state of being beyond abstraction, beyond thought, beyond ego, hopefully to be filled by a shattering insight of life-transforming power. For the Christian, however, the void is not a process of "becoming nothing." Rather, the "Christian void" is founded on a life of self-sacrifice, a self-emptying of all that is false or "void" within us; it is *kenosis*, an emptiness to be filled by God.

The whole purpose of Merton's contemplative life, and ours as well, is to pray for such an emptiness which creates a "place" for God's transfiguring presence. Again, we can think of Saint Paul's expression: "Not I, but Christ lives in me" (Gal 2:20).

When I come I lift my sudden Eucharist

Here is the incarnational heart of the poem. The flower is the Eucharist. It is the inner core, the center of the cactus and emblematic of the Christ within us. Its appearance is "sudden" because it cannot be planned or predicted. Because every epiphany is so sudden, Merton implies the necessity of an exquisite attention to God's omnipresent vestiges.

Christ is within us. Here, the cactus recalls the monstrance that holds the Blessed Sacrament when it is lifted up for Eucharistic adoration. The monstrance is fashioned of precious metal and embedded with jewels; we render God's abode as beautiful as possible. At first thought, the cactus would seem an unlovely monstrance, but its inner blossom renders it beautiful beyond words.

As Christians we live our lives in imitation of Christ, as a monstrance for Christ. By striving to be holy in all our deeds and words, we, the Christ-bearers, proclaim the gospel message to all those who come in contact with us.

Out of the earth's unfathomable joy
Clean and total I obey the world's body

The appearance of the Divine is always a joyful one. The birth of Christ, whose entrance into the world is like the flower of the cactus, brings "unfathomable joy" as well as unfathomable mystery. As the night-flowering cactus is "incarnated" in the "world's body," so does God reveal himself in man: "clean and total..." Christ without sin and complete; God within man.

I am intricate and whole, not art but wrought passion
Excellent deep pleasure of essential waters
Holiness of form and mineral mirth:

The cactus bloom is likened to the Eucharist because like the Bread, it is fresh, symbolic of purity and innocence. The flower is a gift of mother earth whose joy is like any mother's in giving birth. Birth is an act of love and obedience to nature and the flower is its fruit. The flower is "whole," not made from pieces put together (as is a poem), but from passion that originates in the "excellent deep pleasure of essential waters." Without water the flower cannot bloom; it cannot exist, for its "holiness" is one of "form" and "mineral mirth": beauty is married to joy and mirth.

Our birth as Christians began in the "essential waters" of Baptism. Merton felt that poetry returned us to a paradisal, essential state of being. In an essay on the poet Louis Zukofsky, Merton wrote:

> All real valid poetry is a kind of recovery of paradise...the poet...has found his way back to Eden. Here (in the poem) the world gets another chance. Here man, here the reader discovers himself getting another start in life, in hope, in imagination, and why? Hard to say, but probably because the language itself is getting another chance, through the innocence, the teaching, the good faith, the honest senses of the workman poet.[7]

Poetry becomes our garden of Eden where we can regain our childlike sense of wonder and are reborn in the spirit, where we discard all that is false, where we recreate ourselves in the light of Christ's beauty and thus become our true selves.

I am the extreme purity of virginal thirst.

When we think of the Eucharist, we think of Christ's Last Supper. He ate bread and drank wine with the apostles. We also think of the subsequent crucifixion, and Christ's saying "I thirst." Here, the night-flowering cactus reminds us that Christ is the "extreme purity of virginal thirst." Because the innocent Christ enters the night of Gethsemane and drinks the cup of his agony, because he carries his cross and accepts crucifixion, because he drinks bitter vinegar and dies, Merton has Christ saying, "I am the extreme purity of thirst."

Our desire for God is often described in Scripture as a thirst and as a hunger: "Whoever drinks the water I give will never be thirsty again" (Jn 4:14); "He has filled the hungry with good things" (Ps 107:9). Merton thirsted and hungered for "God alone." This thirst and hunger for God was such that he took a vow of "extreme purity," a vow of consecrated chastity. His particular love for God led him to renounce what most people embrace: human love expressed through marriage and forming a family. Everyone, whether single, married or a consecrated religious, deals with loneliness. It is part of the human condition.

But Merton's life had more than the usual share of isolation, anxiety, and self-doubt. He often did not know what God expected of him, but he prayed daily to be shown God's will and he tried to surrender himself to the dark cloud of unknowing.

I neither show my truth nor conceal it
My innocence is descried dimly
Only by divine gift
As a white cavern without explanation.

There is no need for God to "show truth," in the sense that the word "show" implies a willful exhibition to prove, to assert, or to force. Instead, Christ simply said, "I am the Truth." We believe him, but to "see" him is a "divine gift." And if we are gifted with a glimpse of God, he "is descried dimly." He is seen, not in full radiance, but in darkness. Saint Paul says it well: "At present we see indistinctly, as in a mirror" (1 Cor 13:12). The direct vision of God is not for this world. A time will arrive when the dimness will be lifted and there will be no dark cavern, only a "white cavern without explanation."

The white cavern of the night-flowering cactus is *le point vierge* (the central point). Merton says, "The *point vierge* of the spirit—the center of our nothingness where, in apparent despair, one meets God—is found completely in his mercy."[8]

To gaze upon the white loveliness of the night-flowering cactus is to forget ourselves, to surrender ourselves to its beauty. And to gaze upon a poem is to read it in search of its unique loveliness and its inner meaning. The contemplative cannot fully explain God. Neither can the reader fully explain a poem—a poem simply is. However, we can embark on the poet's journey. We can hope to see, hear, taste, touch, and breathe as the poet, to forget ourselves and become one with the poem. Suddenly and briefly the "self" disappears.

There is always a re-appearance of the "self." A poet lost in beauty returns to self and writes the poem in order to share something extraordinary with others. The contemplative who experiences God attempts to share that radiance and writes of that spiritual adventure. Thus we have the great writings of an Augustine, Bonaventure, Bernard, Julian of Norwich, Teresa of Avila, Thérèse of Lisieux, and many others.

We the reader must also "re-appear." Reading a poem, we abide in its light either briefly or for a longer duration. Indeed, sometimes a poem can transform our lives.

We decide to live more deeply, more intensely. We begin to search for beauty in our own lives. Perhaps depression is lifted, or an inner chaos is somewhat stilled, or a fear is dissipated for a time. Perhaps the thirst and hunger for life returns and we seize the day. That momentary detachment from our ego as we partake of some poetry, can be rejuvenating. The scriptural truth that in losing yourself you will find yourself is illustrated. Yet, if someone were to ask us to describe what a poem has done for us, we fall silent. Such an experience is inexpressible.

William James, in his ground breaking *The Varieties of Religious Experience*, offers *ineffability* as one of four characteristics of mystical experience. By this he means that the experience is beyond words because it is essentially indescribable. Direct description being impossible, the mystics and poets settle for an oblique approach and employ the use of symbol or metaphor. And the reader, when asked why a certain poem is a favorite, is often reduced to merely shrugging in response or saying, "Read it and find out for yourself."

He who sees my purity
Dares not speak of it.
When I open once for all my impeccable bell

No one questions my silence:
The all-knowing bird of night flies out of my mouth.

In this stanza we come to a major turn in the poem, when the personal pronoun disappears to be replaced by the third person pronoun "He." When the beholder sees God's radiant purity, he "Dares not speak of it." We are reminded of Christ's transfiguration. Christ along with Peter, John and James went up the mountain to pray.

> While he (Christ) was praying his face changed in appearance and his clothing became dazzling white...Peter and his companions had been overcome by sleep, but becoming fully awake, they saw his glory and...as they were about to part from him, Peter said to Jesus, "Master, it is good that we are here; let us make three tents, one for you, one for Moses, and one for Elijah." But he did not know what he was saying. While he was speaking, a cloud came and cast a shadow over them, and they became frightened when they entered the cloud. Then from the cloud came a voice that said, "This is my chosen Son, listen to him." After the voice had spoken, Jesus was found alone. They fell silent and did not at that time tell anyone what they had seen (Lk 9:28–36).

As the apostles, we fall speechless before God's dazzling beauty. We are silent because words are inadequate. We "dare not speak of it" because we are humbled, realizing full well that we are unworthy to speak of the Holy of Holies. In our silence we imitate that which we behold: "No one questions my silence." The night-flowering cactus simply opens its "impeccable bell." This bell does not ring like an abbey bell, but remains silent. Impeccable (Latin for *peccare*, to sin) because Christ is free from the stain of sin.

As a contemplative whose life is enveloped by silence, Merton would seemingly attempt to embrace greater and greater silence. But the paradox of Merton's life is that he is also a writer. To be true to himself, he had to record his experiences; consequently, he wrote. By sharing his hidden life, he offers us the hope that we too might be blessed with a glimpse of the Divine. He emulates the apostles who first kept Christ's transfiguration hidden until after the Resurrection, when they began to share the good news.

*Have you seen it? Then though my mirth has
  quickly ended
You live forever in its echo:
You will never be the same again.*

A holy sense of God's presence in the midst of our busy lives…surely such a "moment of being" transforms one's life forever. One "will never be the same again."

Merton had a marvelous appreciation of nature. His direct seeing of the sky, clouds, sun, moon, stars, trees, deer, birds, butterflies, and his poetic descriptions of the Kentucky landscape, all illustrate his ability to forget the self in order to behold the beauty around him. He had a great love of flowers and his journals are filled with descriptions of their color, size, shape and unfolding. These gave colorful witness to the grace he received that enabled him to transcend self in order to behold their loveliness.

In a journal entry dated February 4, 1958, Merton wrote:

> Beauty of the sunlight falling on a tall vase of red and white carnations and green leaves on the altar in the novitiate chapel. The light and shade of the red, especially the darkness in the fresh crinkled flower and the light warm red around the darkness, the same color as blood but not "red as blood," utterly unlike blood. Red as a carnation. This flower, this light, this moment, this silence—all, perhaps an illusion, but no matter, for illusion is nevertheless the shadow of reality and reality is the grace that

underlay these lights, these colors, and this silence. The "simplicity" that would have kept those flowers off the altar is, to my mind, less simple than the simplicity which enjoys them there, but does not need them to be there.[9]

In the above prose-poem, Merton says the flower *is* itself, the light *is* itself, and the silence *is* itself, thus Merton realizes that "I am myself." Although he might have preferred that the carnation not be plucked from the earth, Merton perceives the "simplicity" of the beauty because the impulse to place the flower in a vase is not only aesthetic but also charitable. It is a gift to Christ in the tabernacle and to all who behold the flower while praying. "Learn from the way the wild flowers grow" (Mt 6:28–29). How do they grow? Perhaps this may be our perennial mystery, our constant meditation, to be addressed every day of our lives—therein may lie the secret of the inner life.

Merton has, I believe, perceived his own solution to this perennial mystery with his exquisite poem "Night-Flowering Cactus": he sees the flower as symbolizing the way of his own inner life. This cactus flower is not plucked, it is not placed in a vase, it is not used to decorate an altar. It remains rooted in the underground shadows of the earth from which it sprang, and is visible to all those awake and attentive enough to behold its wondrous bloom. Thus, Merton absorbs the flower's lesson as the cactus itself absorbs nourishment from the earth. Then follows the most remarkable unfolding: Merton's flower-poem becomes a poetic icon of prayer passed on to readers willing to take the time to sit and to gaze upon its beauty, and perhaps—through poetry—to learn a lesson from the night-flowering cactus.

Poetry has the potential to unfold life-transfiguring possibilities to us. Poet Stanley Kunitz says, "Through the years I have found this gift of poetry to be life-sustaining, life-enhancing, and absolutely unpredictable. Does one, therefore, live for the sake of poetry? No, the reverse is true: poetry is for the sake of life."[10]

CHAPTER 8

"Stranger"

When no one listens
To the quiet trees
When no one notices
The sun in the pool

Where no one feels
The first drop of rain
Or sees the last star

Or hails the first morning
Of a giant world
Where peace begins
And rages end:

One bird sits still
Watching the work of God:
One turning leaf,

Two falling blossoms,
Ten circles upon the pond.

One cloud upon the hillside,
Two shadows in the valley,
And the light strikes home.

Now dawn commands the capture
Of the tallest fortune,
The surrender
Of no less marvelous prize!

Closer and clearer
Than any wordy master,
Thou inward Stranger
Whom I have never seen,

Deeper and cleaner
Than the clamorous ocean,
Seize up my silence
Hold me in Thy Hand!

Now act is waste
And suffering undone
Laws become prodigals

Limits are torn down
For envy has no property
And passion is none.

Look, the vast Light stands still
Our cleanest Light is One!

CHAPTER 9

"Stranger": A Meditation

The Strange Islands (1957) contains poems that were mostly written in 1955, although a few are from an earlier period. It is a transitional work in which Merton's poetry goes through a transformation. Gone are the didacticism, the rhetoric, the *contemptus mundi* and the florid imagery of his earlier poetry. In their place Merton offers devotion, monastic silence, joy and simplicity; furthermore, he has adopted an ascetic poetic line reminiscent of William Carlos Williams. Merton says of Williams, "I am just beginning to realize how valuable a man Doc Williams was: a great poet and one who developed a new directness of consciousness which I think very salutary."[1]

"New directness" is what renders *The Strange Islands* radiant. Merton envisions both himself and the world with a lucidity that bears the fruit of utterly pure verse. "Stranger" epitomizes his newfound directness.

When no one listens
To the quiet trees
When no one notices
The sun in the pool

We notice the brevity of the poetic line: only a few syllables in each line, similar to the Japanese haiku, a poetic form Merton admired. Merton's ascetic line is also indicative of his new poetic practice: less is more. Merton had become acquainted with this practice when he began his study of Saint John of the Cross. Only in stripping ourselves of all that is egotistical are we prepared for an encounter with the Divine. This spiritual way, of course, influences every aspect of Merton's life. He strips his poetry to a point that can only be described as minimalist. Merton commentator Thérèse Lentfoehr refers to this poetry as "Zen Transparencies," and describes *The Strange Islands* as, verses of "naked simplicity and directness."[2]

The opening setting of "Stranger" is obviously pastoral; indeed, few of Merton's poems have an urban background. Merton suggests that nature serves as a model of being. If we emulate nature's way, we fulfill our purpose which is to *be* our true selves. He begins this poem with the sense of hearing, not surprising because the longer

Merton remained a monk, the more he realized the paramount importance of "listening" as a central practice in the contemplative life. He exhorts us to listen to the trees and to "notice the sun in the pool" because he feels that "no one listens" and no one takes time to "notice."

Trees and sunlight are both nature's ever-present bounty, but if we do not take notice, then we cannot be touched or drawn into the radiance of these gifts. Thus we are absent from some of life's treasures. True, if we don't listen and notice and appreciate nature's beauty, it is still there as it has been from time immemorial, but we have missed a precious opportunity.

A sense of our separation from beauty is the subliminal criticism made by the poem; yet this separation can be mended simply by taking time, especially to hear the voice of God—in the trees, the rustling of leaves in the wind, in one another....

Where no one feels
The first drop of rain
Or sees the last star

To take the time to feel the rain is advised by other poets as well. William Wordsworth warned against "getting and spending" and to laying "waste our powers"; he exhorts us to embrace God's beautiful world as our inher-

itance. William Carlos Williams loved the rain and encouraged us to not only listen to it, but to venture into it without an umbrella, to feel the rain fall on our eyelids, on our lips, to allow ourselves to be drenched. In short, to enjoy the utter abandonment to the Now Moment and to the joy of falling, splashing rain.

Merton is preparing us, however, for another kind of abandonment: abandonment to God, which can bring us our greatest joy. But to ready ourselves for such abandonment, Merton reminds us that we must be attentive even to small, seemingly "insubstantial" things, like raindrops. If we listen carefully, we will indeed hear the rainfall, as did Merton in his hermitage.

In his exquisite prose poem "Rain and the Rhinoceros," Merton listens to the rain because "it reminds me again and again that the whole world runs by rhythms I have not yet learned to recognize."[3] And in the rhythm of his verse, now stripped bare so that one is not diverted by anything extraneous, we are told to observe the "last star" to keep ourselves attentive until morning, as it were.

The first two stanzas stress the quality of our awareness. We must become friendly with the world. We must not be a stranger to God's gifts; we must not be alienated from them.

Or hails the first morning
Of a giant world
Where peace begins
And rages end:

How few people rise early enough in the morning to hail the beauty of the sunrise. Too many of us are strangers not only to the sunrise but also to morning peace. The poet Wallace Stevens observes, "Wine and music are not good until the afternoon. But poetry is like prayer in that it is most effective in…the times of solitude as, for example, in the earliest morning."[4] Trappists like Merton understand the spiritual resonance of the sunrise and the rarefied ambiance of the morning—they rise at 3:00 A.M. for the first of the liturgical hours of prayer.

One bird sits still
Watching the work of God:
One turning leaf,
Two falling blossoms
Ten circles upon the pond.

When one is fresh and attentive to the glory of the morning, one is able to focus upon singular beauty. Notice how the poet enumerates the surrounding beauty:

"one bird," "one turning leaf," "two falling blossoms," "ten circles upon the pond." This kind of tunnel vision appreciates the small, singular aspects of nature, those diminutives that we too often fail to see. Spiritually speaking, we must begin with the small. Later, we will appreciate the larger vision.

This kind of aesthetic is also indicative of Merton's interest in all things Japanese: calligraphy, haiku, the tea ceremony and, of course, Zen Buddhism. In the West we are prone to fill a vase with a profusion of flowers. But the Japanese delicately place one flower in a vase. In the tea ceremony, one *objet d'art* is passed around for each person to hold, to examine, to relish. To understand this singular focusing of one's attention is to comprehend the spiritual direction toward which Merton was headed in the mid- to late-1950s.

Again, focusing on one or two aspects of nature's beauty is a spiritual discipline that brings us before "the work of God." Closely observing the outside world is a paradigm for soul-watching. If we look upon the bird, the leaf, the blossoms, and the circles of water, we cannot help being reminded of God's omnipresence and love.

Merton's love of silence and solitude, his yearning

for a hermitage, demonstrate his spiritual preference. Abiding in a hermitage can lead to a life bared of all that is extraneous, as if based on Thoreau's dictum: "Simplify! Simplify! Simplify!" The ultimate diminishment is to reduce our contact with others and this is what all hermits do in following their singular call to devote themselves to God alone—being alone with the Alone.

Merton's aesthetic sense has been sharpened. He learns not to succumb to seeing the woods, but to see the trees. This ability to zero-in on life is certainly the result of his Trappist asceticism, but it also shows the influence of his study of Zen, and its emphasis on focused attention.

Merton as a poet spent much of his life striving for a state of wonder, experienced first during his adolescent years in England when he read the Romantic poets. In "Stranger," Merton succeeds in regaining this wonder because he is a poet and contemplative who accepts the fact that he lives in the world. The world is everything we know through our senses; it is our home; we can't "fall off" the earth. We also know it is not our permanent home; it is the sacred place where we work out our life in God. As a professed religious, Merton understood that living a godly life doesn't rule out our appreciation of a world "charged with the grandeur of God."[5] In fact, the more we are in harmony with God's grandeur the more we are likely to do his will. For always before us is nature, "being itself" by following God's will.

One cloud upon the hillside,
Two shadows in the valley
And the light strikes home.

Now dawn commands the capture
Of the tallest fortune,
The surrender
Of no less marvelous prize!

Like the poet Walt Whitman, Merton catalogues nature's bounty as, "one cloud," "two shadows," "the light," "the dawn," "the tallest fortune." He prepares us to surrender all this beauty for a "no less marvelous prize!" Notice the exclamation mark at the end of this stanza. It marks the end of the first half of the poem that dealt with landscape. We now enter another plane: soul-scape. A "marvelous prize" piques us. What could be more marvelous than the beauty of nature? To find out, we continue to surrender to the poem.

Surrendering ourselves to a poem is akin to the spiritual way of Jesuit Jean-Pierre de Caussade who wrote about surrender in *Abandonment to Divine Providence.*

Caussade encourages us to bow reverently to "the sacrament of the present moment" which according to him provides "an ever-flowing source of holiness."[6]

Closer and clearer
Than any wordy master,
Thou inward Stranger
Whom I have never seen,

We now focus our attention on the "inward Stranger" who is "Closer and clearer / Than any wordy master." Merton addresses his inner true self, which is Christ. Christ is closer and clearer than anyone else to the poet, even closer to him than he is to himself. The reference to a "wordy master" is a reference to Merton the poet. Merton has indeed mastered the poetic form, but even though his poetry is now stripped, it is still "too wordy." Any description of Christ ultimately falls short because Christ is ineffable.

Merton cannot, however, accept complete silence when it comes to Christ. As a poet he must obey the impulse to capture all that is beautiful in his life. To fail to attempt describing the Divine is to reject the *Logos*. Such avoidance would be tantamount to burying one's light, one's talent, for a poet is gifted by God with the ability to hint at such divine beauty.

We have not *seen* Christ with our eyes, but we meet him through the Gospel. Yet too often, as Merton suggests, Christ is a stranger to us. We fail to recognize him, to see him, to touch him. This is the result, not so much of our sinfulness, but of our inability to be attentive to his presence. We are like the apostles in the Garden of Gethsemane: we fall asleep while Christ is with us. Our inattention or lack of awareness, however, doesn't nullify presence. He is with us still.

Deeper and cleaner
Than the clamorous ocean,
Seize up my silence
Hold me in Thy Hand!

Merton personifies the inner self: the Stranger. To meet the Stranger, one must plunge into the deepest self, which is "Deeper and cleaner / Than the clamorous ocean." The poet is aware of the Stranger, but he is not yet one with the Stranger: "Hold me in Thy Hand!" The exclamation mark underscores the poet's poignant longing to be one with God. He prays to be held in the hand of the Divine. He is silent; he waits. This is the place of surrender. Duality now waits for Unity. Profusion is diminished, and enumeration disappears into zero, into the nothingness of the void, toward the moment of encounter with the Stranger, the true self.

Now act is waste
And suffering undone
Laws become prodigals

Limits are torn down
For envy has no property
And passion is none.

As already mentioned, Merton was well versed in the poetry and drama of T. S. Eliot. This stanza echoes Eliot's play *Murder in the Cathedral*. Eliot has his character, Archbishop Thomas Becket, articulate his newly won wisdom, "Acting is suffering / And suffering is action." To go beyond action and suffering, according to Becket, one must surrender to the still center of the turning wheel, to the place of "eternal patience," which is the Divine will.

Merton concurs: "act is waste" and "suffering is undone." Neither act nor suffering brings us into the presence of the Divine. Neither does "Laws" and "Limits." If we obey all laws and subject ourselves to all "Limits," such obedience still does not render us worthy of God. "Envy" and "passion" of any kind are also useless. So what is one to do? The answer: nothing. Or rather, just be yourself. And when you are your true self, you will see and become one with the Light of the world.

Look, the vast Light stands still
Our cleanest Light is One!

Notice the play on words: by being yourself, you have *won* (*One!*), and victory is granted forever. Notice also how the poem begins with "no one" and concludes with "One!" Clearly, Merton's message is that, in order to know the Stranger within, we must acknowledge our own nothingness, our "no one-ness."

For a prose description of what it means to encounter the *point vierge* as described in the poem "Stranger," we need only read the following:

> The first chirps of the waking day birds mark the *point vierge* of the dawn under a sky as yet without real light, a moment of awe and inexpressible innocence, when the Father in perfect silence opens their eyes. They begin to speak to Him, not with fluent song, but with an awakening question that is their dawn state, their state at the *point vierge*. Their condition asks if it is time for them to "be." He answers "yes." Then, they one by one wake up and become birds.[7]

We, too, are called to be our true selves. This requires an attentive awakening, during which we wholeheartedly agree to become ourselves and give our joyful assent answered by the Father's eternal, affirmative "Yes."

CHAPTER 10

Ten Steps to Reading
Poetry in a Holy Way

1. *Choose your verse well.*

Read poetry that has been handed down as classic. This will develop your ability (and taste) to differentiate between poetry that is great and that which will surely not pass the test of time. Read contemporary poetry as well. Good libraries keep their poetry shelves full, so only purchase poetry volumes when you are certain that this is verse that you will want to revisit.

2. *Know your poet's life.*

Although it is not absolutely necessary to know the poet's biography in detail, I suggest that this knowledge often enhances the appreciation for a poet's verse. For instance, knowledge of Francis Thompson's lifelong battle with an opium addiction certainly assists the reader in penetrating the more obscure lines of *The Hound of Heaven*. Knowledge of Merton's struggle to integrate his contemplative and poetic self increases an appreciation of his poetic nuances.

3. Take it with you!

Poetry can travel with you. Bring your favorite poems with you wherever you go, even while walking, jogging, or during your daily business of life. How often do you find yourself waiting in offices for appointments, for friends or for a bus, plane or train? Read your favorite poems during such times. They are food for the mind and soul. Time spent with poetry is not wasted but sanctified.

4. Repeat your favorite lines.

"Center" with your favorite verse: if possible, repeat it aloud and allow the verse to sink down into your soul. Poetry can often render us calm, hopeful, energized, and soul-lifted.

5. Surrender your imagination!

You are a co-creator with the poet. What you bring to a poem—your insight, your interpretation, your imagining—is unique. Your engagement with a poem is *once in time*, never to be repeated by you or by anyone else. So do not be afraid to surrender to a poem: it may be the very poem that transforms!

6. Open yourself to the unknown.

Reading a poem is like embarking upon a journey; thus, every reader becomes a pilgrim. Pilgrims visit holy shrines to touch the sacred ground where Christ walked or where a saint lived or died. In such holy places they, too, hope to be touched by God. Be open to such possibility when you engage a poem. To prepare yourself for such an experience, you need only offer up a simple prayer: "Lord, speak to me through this poem."

7. Practice the art of attention.

Over and over I have mentioned how important it is to be attentive to a poem. Read it carefully, every word, every line, notice every comma, every period. Ignore nothing. Even the type style and the spacing of verse and stanza may offer clues about its meaning. We sometimes must dig to find the gold of life, and attentive reading is like digging, not the kind that exhausts and sullies, but the kind that lifts and radiates.

8. Let poetry into your heart!

Create your own oratory of the heart. The "open sesame" to the door of this oratory is poetry. When you read and pray a poem, you enter upon a plane that is described by poets and mystics as the contemplative state. Poetry's imagery possesses the power to take you beyond the imagery itself to the ineffable, to that which can only be described as spiritual.

9. Keep a poetry notebook.

It is helpful, as recommended by poetry critic Helen Vendler, to write out your favorite poems in your own hand. It is extraordinary how a poem will unfold its beauty and inner truth when copied in your own handwriting. The notebook can also be used to write down reflections and insights; thus, you create a unique "Psalter" for spiritual nourishment, available whenever you need it.

10. Share!

If a poem has soul-lifted you, it may do the same for others. I have always shared poems that have moved or inspired me. Many students and friends have thanked me for a poem that contained a "saving word" for them, too. Perhaps a poem has been sent to you for the sole purpose of your becoming an instrument to make known its presence. I think of Jane Kenyon's volume, *Otherwise,* that many people who suffer from depression have discovered. Jane Kenyon's verse has brought much solace and hope into the lives of thousands. Sharing poetry thus becomes an act of love.

Suggested Poems for Prayer

Berrigan, Daniel
The Crucifix
Facing It

Berry, Wendell
The Way of Pain
Sabbaths: 1985 III

Brother Antoninus
The Kiss of the Cross

Cairnes, Scott
The More Earnest Prayer of Christ

Chesterton, G. K.
The Donkey

Craig, David
"Christ Bearing the Cross" by El Greco
Gethsemane

Powers, Jessica
  Without Beauty
  Humility
  The Moment After Suffering
  Advent

Quenon, OCSO, Paul
  Terrors of Paradise

Rilke, Rainer Maria
  The Raising of Lazarus
  The Olive Garden

Robinson, Edwin Arlington
  The Prodigal Son

Schuyler, James
  I sit down to type

Seitz, Ron
  The Gethsemani Poems

Sexton, Anne
  Is It True?

Sitwell, Edith
  The Canticle to the Rose

Villa, José Garcia
   My most. My most. O my Lost!

Wilkinson, Rosemary
   Mother Mary

Wright, Charles
   Lives of the Saints
   Jesuit Graves

Wright, OSB, Ralph
   Leaves of Water

Zagajewski, Adam
   Mysticism for Beginners

Notes

Introduction

1. Robinson Jeffers, *The Selected Letters of Robinson Jeffers*, ed. by Ann N. Ridgeway (John Hopkins Press, 1968), p. 225.

2. George Steiner, *Errata* (New Haven: Yale University Press, 1998), p. 27.

Chapter 1
Poetry as Contemplative Prayer

1. Thomas Kelly, *A Testament of Devotion* (New York: Harper and Brothers, 1941), p. 29.

2. Michael Casey, *Sacred Reading, The Ancient Art of Lectio Divina* (Liguori, MI, Liguori Publications, 1998), p. 83.

3. Pope John Paul II, *Letter to Artists* (Boston: Pauline Books & Media, 1999), p. 20.

4. Ibid., p. 16.

5. Ibid., p. 18.

6. Ibid., p. 33.

Chapter 2
Thomas Merton: Monk and Poet

1. Thomas Merton, *The Seven Storey Mountain* (New York: Harcourt, Brace and Co., 1948), p. 73.

2. Simone Weil, *The Simone Weil Reader: A Legendary Spiritual Odyssey of Our Time* (New York: David McKay, 1977), p. 379.

3. Thomas Merton, *The Seven Storey Mountain* (New York: Harcourt, Brace and Co., 1948), p. 111.

4. Thomas Merton, *Seeds of Destruction* (New York: Farrar, Straus, Giroux, 1964), pp. 274–275.

5. Thomas Merton, *The Seven Storey Mountain* (New York: Harcourt, Brace and Co., 1948), p. 325.

6. Thomas Merton, *Conjectures of a Guilty Bystander* (New York: Doubleday, 1966), pp. 140–141.

7. Thomas Merton, *The Asian Journal of Thomas Merton* (New York: New Directions, 1973), p. 233.

Chapter 3
From Merton's Pen

1. Paul Wilkes, "American Scribe," *Boston College Magazine.* Winter, 1999, pp. 30–37.

2. Thomas Merton, *Seeds of Contemplation* (New York: New Directions, 1949), p. 28.

3. Ibid., p. 28.

4. Ibid., p. 41.

5. Paul Wilkes, "American Scribe," *Boston College Magazine.* Winter, 1999, pp. 30–37.

6. Thomas Merton, *No Man Is an Island* (New York: Doubleday), p. 133.

7. Ibid., p. 33.

8. Thomas Merton, *Thoughts in Solitude* (New York: Farrar, Straus, Giroux, 1956), p. 85.

9. Ibid., p. 62.

10. Ibid., p. 117.

11. Thomas Merton, *Bread in the Wilderness* (New York: New Directions, 1953), p. 3.

12. Ibid., p. 3.

13. Ibid., p. 54.

14. Ibid., p. 43.

15. Ibid., p. 14.

16. Thomas Merton, "Poetry and Contemplation: A Reappraisal," in *The Literary Essays of Thomas Merton*. Brother Patrick Hart, ed. (New York: New Directions, 1981), p. 346.

17. Ibid. p. 346.

18. Ibid., p. 347.

19. Thomas Merton, *The New Man* (New York: Farrar, Straus, Giroux, 1961), p. 85.

20. Robert Faggen, ed., *Striving Towards Being: The Letters of Thomas Merton and Czeslaw Milosz* (New York: Farrar, Straus, Giroux, 1997), pp. 54–55.

21. Sandra M. Gilbert, *Acts of Attention: The Poems of D. H. Lawrence* (Southern Illinois University Press, 1990), p. 5.

22. Thomas Merton, *New Seeds of Contemplation* (New York: New Directions, 1961), p. 1.

23. Thomas Merton, *Conjectures of a Guilty Bystander* (New York: Doubleday, 1966), pp.135–136.

24. Pope John Paul II, *Letter to Artists* (Boston: Pauline Books & Media, 1999), p. 4.

Chapter 5
"Elias–Variations on a Theme": A Meditation

1. William H. Shannon, *Thomas Merton's Dark Path* (New York: Farrar, Straus, Giroux, 1981), p. 169.

2. Jonathan Montaldo, forthcoming volume, *Loving Winter When the Plant Says Nothing: Thomas Merton's Spirituality in His Private Journals*, pp. 11–12.

3. George Kilcourse, *Ace of Freedoms* (Notre Dame: University of Notre Dame Press, 1993), p. 225.

4. Thomas Merton, *A Search for Solitude* (San Francisco: HarperCollins, 1996), p. 14.

5. Thomas Merton, *Disputed Questions* (New York: Harcourt and Brace, 1985), p. 189.

6. Thomas Merton, *Turning Toward the World: The Pivotal Years*, *The Merton Journals*, *vol. 4*. Victor Kramer, ed. (San Francisco: HarperCollins, 1996), p. 87.

7. Thomas Merton, *Life and Holiness* (New York: Image Books, 1963), p. 9.

8. Ibid., p. 24.

9. Ibid., p. 112.

10. Ibid., p. 112.

11. Thomas Merton, *A Search for Solitude.* Lawrence Cunningham, ed. (San Francisco: HarperCollins, 1996), pp. 214–215.

Chapter 7
"Night-Flowering Cactus": A Meditation

1. George Kilcourse, *Ace of Freedoms: Thomas Merton's Christ* (Notre Dame: University of Notre Dame Press, 1995), p. 74.

2. Thomas Merton, *The Hidden Ground of Love* (New York: Farrar, Straus, Giroux, 1985), pp. 63–64.

3. Thomas Merton, *Conjectures of a Guilty Bystander* (New York: Doubleday, 1966), p. 142.

4. Thomas Merton, *Seeds of Contemplation* (New York: New Directions, 1949), p. 29.

5. Ibid.

6. Ibid.

7. Thomas Merton, *The Literary Essay of Thomas Merton.* Brother Patrick Hart, ed. (New York: New Directions, 1985), p. 128.

8. Thomas Merton, *A Search for Solitude* (San Francisco: HarperSanFrancisco, 1996), p. 164.

9. Thomas Merton, *Conjectures of a Guilty Bystander* (New York: Doubleday, 1966), p. 151.

10. Stanley Kunitz, *Passing Through: The Later Poems* (New York: W. W. Norton, 1995), p. 12.

Chapter 9
"Stranger": A Meditation

1. Thomas Merton, *The Road to Joy: Letters to New and Old Friends.* Robert Daggy, ed. (New York: Farrar, Straus, Giroux, 1989), p. 257.

2. Sister Thérèse Lentfoehr, *Words and Silence: On the Poetry of Thomas Merton* (New York: New Directions, 1979), p. 55.

3. Thomas Merton, *Raids on the Unspeakable* (New York: New Directions, 1964), p. 9.

4. Charles M. Murphy, *Wallace Stevens: A Spiritual Poet in a Secular Age* (New York: Paulist Press, 1997), p. 2.

5. Oscar Williams, ed. *Immortal Poems of the English Language* (New York: Simon Schuster, 1952), p. 458.

6. Jean-Pierre de Caussade, *Abandonment to Divine Providence* (New York: Image Books, 1975), p. 16.

7. Thomas Merton, *Conjectures of a Guilty Bystander* (New York: Doubleday Image, 1968), p. 131.

Robert Waldron teaches high school poetry and literature at Boston Latin School in Massachusetts, and is a frequent lecturer on Thomas Merton's life and writings. He is the author of another volume in this series, *Poetry As Prayer: The Hound of Heaven*, and has published numerous magazine articles on poetry, literature and religion.

Pauline
BOOKS & MEDIA

The Daughters of St. Paul operate book and media centers at the following addresses. Visit, call or write the one nearest you today, or find us on the World Wide Web, www.pauline.org

CALIFORNIA
3908 Sepulveda Blvd., Culver City, CA 90230; 310-397-8676
5945 Balboa Ave., San Diego, CA 92111; 858-565-9181
46 Geary Street, San Francisco, CA 94108; 415-781-5180

FLORIDA
145 S.W. 107th Ave., Miami, FL 33174; 305-559-6715

HAWAII
1143 Bishop Street, Honolulu, HI 96813; 808-521-2731
Neighbor Islands call: 800-259-8463

ILLINOIS
172 North Michigan Ave., Chicago, IL 60601; 312-346-4228

LOUISIANA
4403 Veterans Memorial Blvd., Metairie, LA 70006; 504-887-7631

MASSACHUSETTS
Rte. 1, 885 Providence Hwy., Dedham, MA 02026; 781-326-5385

MISSOURI
9804 Watson Rd., St. Louis, MO 63126; 314-965-3512

NEW JERSEY
561 U.S. Route 1, Wick Plaza, Edison, NJ 08817; 732-572-1200

NEW YORK
150 East 52nd Street, New York, NY 10022; 212-754-1110
78 Fort Place, Staten Island, NY 10301; 718-447-5071

OHIO
2105 Ontario Street (at Prospect Ave.), Cleveland, OH 44115; 216-621-9427

PENNSYLVANIA
9171-A Roosevelt Blvd., Philadelphia, PA 19114; 215-676-9494

SOUTH CAROLINA
243 King Street, Charleston, SC 29401; 843-577-0175

TENNESSEE
4811 Poplar Ave., Memphis, TN 38117 901-761-2987

TEXAS
114 Main Plaza, San Antonio, TX 78205; 210-224-8101

VIRGINIA
1025 King Street, Alexandria, VA 22314; 703-549-3806

CANADA
3022 Dufferin Street, Toronto, Ontario, Canada M6B 3T5; 416-781-9131
1155 Yonge Street, Toronto, Ontario, Canada M4T 1W2; 416-934-3440

¡También somos su fuente para libros, videos y música en español!